THE BOOK OF
LOVE

THE BOOK OF
LOVE

DAPHNE ROSE KINGMA

Foreword by M. J. Ryan,
author of *Attitudes of Gratitude*

MJF BOOKS
NEW YORK

Published by MJF Books
Fine Communications
Two Lincoln Square
60 West 66th Street
New York, NY 10023

The Book of Love
LC Control Number 2001098734
ISBN 1-56731-485-6

This edition published by arrangement with Conari Press.

Cover design: Ame Beanland
Book design: Suzanne Albertson

Manufactured in the United States of America on acid-free paper

MJF Books and the MJF colophon are trademarks of Fine Creative
Media, Inc.

VB   10   9   8   7   6   5   4   3   2   1

FOR *Dearest Chris,*

sister on the path
    through all life's sacred journeys

THE BOOK OF
LOVE

Foreword

by M. J. Ryan, author of *Attitudes of Gratitude*
and *The Giving Heart*

A COURSE IN LOVING

I have had the very great honor of knowing and working with Daphne Rose Kingma for the past twenty-two years, and can think of no one better to have written something called *The Book of Love*. Indeed, it is not an exaggeration for me to say that most of what I know about love I learned from Daphne, and her teachings inform all that I have written about gratitude, generosity, and happiness.

Some of us, like me, write in order to learn something, to become someone finer; for others, like Daphne, their work is a written reflection of the essence of who they are. I always say, as a way of introducing her to folks who have never met her, that Daphne is an angel, an ethereal presence sent to Earth to show us how to love one another better. She does this through her very being, in all of her nine books, and, most particularly, here in *The Book of Love,* a compilation of the best of her advice from *True Love* and *A Lifetime of Love.*

I am very excited that this collection has been published. In your hand, you are holding the most profound perspective on sustaining a loving relationship that I have ever encountered. Its core teachings—that love is both an emotional and a spiritual experience, and that, in Daphne's words, "love is a process, not a destination"—are are easy to lose track of in the pick-up-your-socks and where-were-you-last-night? ordinariness of daily life. But nothing short of that broad perspective is needed when we are trying to enact the full magnitude of our lovingness on the human level, day in and day out. For we as individuals exist on the material, emotional, and the spiritual planes, and our relationships do too. To keep love alive, we must deal not only with who takes the garbage out, but also how we trigger one another's wounds from the past, and what we need to do to raise the consciousness of our love so that it is a reflection of our highest and best selves.

This is no small task. I don't know about you, but I make mistakes in my relationships daily. I get impatient, forget to be grateful for the other person's presence in my life, get hung up on the domestic details—"He said he was going to send that package FedEx and he forgot"—lose my temper, am too tired to connect physically . . . the list goes on and on. That's why I treasure *The Book of Love.* Here, in a series of short, extremely practical yet profound writings, are ways to raise the consciousness of your relationship, to get it off the petty plane it can get stuck on and make it the best it can possibly be, for yourself and for your beloved. Some of these essays remind us of things we know but lose sight of; others are perspectives or behaviors that may be new. Taken all together, they give us a blueprint for developing our capacity to love and be loved to its utmost. And what is more important than that? For as Daphne has so eloquently written, "In the end, nothing we do or say in this lifetime will matter as much as the way we have loved one another."

May our loving ripple out into the world in ever-expanding circles.

More Love

*H*aving a relationship is about loving and being loved, feeling preciously and deliciously connected to another human being, having a place for your heart to come home to.

Creating this homestead for your heart is stunningly simple and amazingly complex. It's simple because we fall in love so easily, and falling in love feels wonderful. It's complex because *we* are complex. Each of us is a fascinating weave of personality and soul. We are human beings alive and loving in life as we know it, with time, human limitations, and real circumstances as our traveling companions. We are also eternal spiritual beings who have stepped onto the human stage for a moment to taste of the exquisite pleasures and learn the soul-honing lessons that life on Earth has to teach. In this world, life is the school, love is the lesson, and our many-faceted relationships the teachers. Indeed, more than anything else we undertake in this life, our intimate relationships are, for each of us, the pilgrimage to our own capacity to love.

Whenever we create this thing we call "a relationship," we are meeting another person in several dimensions at once. On the spiritual level we are fulfilling a soul agreement; that is, an ancient promise made before we were born in the realm of the spirit to meet with another person in this life and engage in a relationship that would expand our soul's experience of love. But we also love as personalities, as people with families and histories, heartaches and grudges, talents and aspirations, dashed dreams and unexpected miracles. In personality, we live what we think of as ordinary life, raising children, having houses, paying bills, being young, and getting old. In this arena our tender human feelings arise, express themselves in the habits and interactions that both delight and irritate our partners, show us more and more who we are, and help us transform ourselves and the persons we have chosen to love.

We are both emotional *and* spiritual beings, and it is both of these aspects, side by side but moving generally in the same direction, like the two shining rails of a train track, that keep moving us forward toward more and more love. Sometimes loving more is attained through loss and sorrow, sometimes through ravishing joy and pleasure, sometimes through the quiet steady passage through a life of days. Whatever the specifics of the journey, two human beings, both personality and soul, join up for a time and, through their conjunction *in relationship,* each of them grows in their own capacity to love.

In order to fashion our relationships so they can give us more love and so we can become more loving, we must remember that both of these dimensions are constantly at play and that both of them need to be nurtured, educated, and supported. This is not only so we can have more satisfying relationships in the day-to-day and here-and-now. It is also so that our souls, those eternally blossoming flowers, can fulfill their timeless, endless yearning for an ever-more-encompassing experience of love.

That's why, when you have a relationship, you need to be aware of what your personality is doing— and learn the behaviors that will bring you and your beloved harmony, satisfaction, and closeness on an emotional level. And it is why you must also hold the awareness that a relationship is your soul's undertaking and recognize that your soul has chosen this particular person and this particular relationship experience to further expand your capacity for love.

There are great rewards for this.

The more we practice the disciplines of our emotional selves, the more wonderful our relationships will be in a daily coming-home-to-the-hearth sort of way. We will be happier; we will be grateful to love one another; we will find solace, comfort, passion, and friendship in one another's presence; our hearts will be glad. And the more we practice the disciplines of spiritual awareness, the more our relationships will be havens for our spirits. They will be continual reminders of the majesty of our spiritual essence; in this they will cause our souls to rejoice.

The Book of Love is a guidebook to both of these realms. If you're having difficulty in just plain getting through your daily emotional life, read from the part called "The Emotional Path to Love" to find a way to deepen your connection and make it sweeter and more gracious. If you've lost sight of your purpose together, the deeper meaning of your connection, or if you've become complacent, conducting your relationship on only the level of emotional interchange, read from "The Spiritual Journey to Love" to be reminded once again of the sacred magnitude of your union. You can read the entire book in progression as a pathway to growth, or let it fall open in your hands to gently guide you in a new direction.

The Book of Love is a gift to your love, a prayer that your relationship will open and expand, and that through it both you and your beloved will become more spiritually alive and emotionally fulfilled. It comes to you with my love.

Daphne Rose Kingma

PART I

The Emotional Path to Love

Feel your way into love.

Let your emotions mark out the path.

Your heart knows the way.

You will surely get there.

Discovering Your Loving Self, Treasuring Your Beloved

_____

How can we love one another if we
have not first loved ourselves?
How can we find the path to that
other's heart without holding our
own heart in a basket of tender care?

We ourselves are the measure of the love we
can deliver, the beauty of the love that
we can share.

LOVE YOURSELF

*A*ll too many of us consider love to be the miracle by which, finally, we will become complete human beings. This is the fixer-upper notion of love, the idea that we're not all right as we are but if we can just get loved by somebody, then that will prove we're OK.

Ironically, however, in order to be well loved, you need first to love yourself. For, in love, we get not necessarily what we deserve, but what we *think* we deserve. Just as Harry Homeowner who has a house that's worth $1 million might sell it for only $500,000 if that's all he thinks it's worth, so the person who underestimates his or her own value will always be shortchanged in love.

Love begets love. If you don't think well of yourself, you can't be positively affected by the person who is celebrating you for a specialness you don't believe you have. If you don't know, and love, what's important, special, precious, and beautiful about yourself, you can be sure you will not be serenaded, sent roses, lauded, paraded, or daily smothered in kisses by someone who does.

Loving yourself is knowing yourself, enjoying and valuing the person that you are, and understanding that self-knowledge is a lifelong personal enterprise. It means that you appreciate yourself at least as much as you value your honey, that you know he or she is as lucky in love as you believe you are. It means you measure your strengths and weaknesses neither with the abuse of self-deprecation nor the insanity of egomania, but with genuineness, with accuracy. Loving yourself is recognizing your gifts and talents and putting them to good use, acknowledging your flaws and forgiving yourself for them. Loving yourself is reaching for more, for the best, in you.

So often we put up with shabby treatment in love because we don't believe we deserve better. But self-love is always the model for the love you may reasonably expect, the true measure of the love you will give and get. Your heart can only hold as much love as you believe it can. So treat yourself better, believe you deserve to be treated well, and you will get treated ever more wonderfully in love. Love yourself! ☺

SAY WHAT YOU FEEL

*F*eelings reside in us like a river and pass through our consciousness in an ever-moving flow. They range from fear, sadness, shame, and anger to joy, delight, exuberance, and playfulness. At any moment, we can reach in and discover what we're feeling. Saying what you feel is giving audible language to the flow of feelings, discovering and articulating the emotions that are the constant undercurrent of our lives.

Revealing these emotional tides to the person you love is a way for you to continue to endear yourself to your partner. We often think that intimacy is created merely by falling in love or by what we do, plan, buy, or pursue together. But it is actually getting to know another person through the intricate texture of his or her emotions that makes us feel truly connected. In fact, an intimate relationship at its core is a process of trading feelings to a high degree.

Paradoxically and sadly, it's often when we love someone that we tend not to share our emotions and to revert to information-laden conversation. It just doesn't occur to us that the other person is interested in what we are sad, happy, scared, or angry about. In this way, surprisingly, proximity can breed not intimacy but a sense of isolation.

Believe it or not, it's the experience of knowing you that your beloved wants. He or she wants to see the kaleidoscope of your inner emotional contents, to understand how you feel, to discover what makes you tick. It's all this that makes you who you are, that makes you uniquely lovable.

If it's difficult for you to express your emotions, you need to know that it will be worth it to step into these unfamiliar waters and discover the treasures at your depths. Not only will your partner be pleased to connect with you, but the experience of discovering your feelings will give you a greater sense of the richness of your own inner life. So, let the person you love enter the underground stream of your feelings so he can cherish you, so she can love you even more, by starting to say, exactly and always, whatever is in your heart and mind. ♡

ASK FOR WHAT
YOU NEED

*A*sking for what you need is just that: stating that there is something amiss about which you need some care or response. "Would you please close the window? I'm freezing." "I need you to hold me; I'm scared." "Will you give me a back rub? My shoulder hurts." "Can you skip the ball game and go to the movies with me? I've been home alone all day and I'm stir-crazy."

Asking for what we need is such a simple yet difficult thing that most of us rarely, if ever, do it. In fact, it is so hard (or easy) that most of us would rather try almost anything else than to ask quite simply and directly for precisely what we need. We would rather presume that our sweetheart will know without our telling or hope that in time our spouse will, by osmosis, figure it out. Often, we'd just as soon give up on getting the thing we need than to actually have to ask for it.

We don't like to ask because we think of asking as revealing neediness—which is precisely what it is. Asking means we are in a vulnerable state and that we are hoping the other person will care enough to minister to us in our pitiful, imperfect, and inadequate condition.

Unfortunately, when we're in love we can get into the strange frame of mind that somehow we ought to be perfect and invulnerable. It's as if we believe that one of the requirements of love is that only people who need absolutely nothing can be loved. In reality, love ministers to our vulnerabilities, and the gift of love is that it can do for us what we are unable to do for ourselves.

Asking for what you need reveals the true fragileness of your humanity and invites the person who loves you to expand the range of his or her own. Responding to a stated request not only gives the needy person the relief of having the need fulfilled, but it also gives the giver a sense of being able to be effective, to offer a gift of value. On these occasions, you are both enjoined to expand the range of your love and your humanity.

However, just because you ask for something doesn't necessarily mean that you will get it. Asking in itself doesn't guarantee results—you may ask your spouse to buy you a Porsche, but that doesn't mean he or she has the wherewithal to provide it. When you're just learning to ask, not getting positive results can be discouraging. Just remember that asking does greatly improve your chances; the more you ask, the better the odds are that you will get what you need and want. ☙

BE EMOTIONALLY BRAVE

$\mathcal{A}$ lot of us are emotional chickens, afraid to communicate what we're feeling, afraid that what we disclose will be ignored, made fun of, or ridiculed. So rather than taking the risk of spitting it out—whatever it is—we just keep quiet. Or even defend our emotionally shutdown stance, saying that talking about feelings never does any good anyway.

Being an emotional chicken has old, sad origins. It begins when we aren't listened to as children, when we were told that the things we said were unimportant, or sensed that no one was feeling with us in our private anguish. Feeling that way made us scared, and taught us to keep our thoughts and feelings to ourselves. But emotions kept in, stuffed down, or anaesthetized in various ways always take an emotional toll on us.

Being emotionally brave on the other hand means that in spite of the possible adverse effects, you will risk saying the things that may leave you feeling exposed and trust that your partner will hear you.

Lana was afraid to tell Ron that she had been sexually abused as a child. She was terrified that he would be disgusted and reject her. Instead, when she finally worked up the nerve to tell him, he held her very tenderly and told her how sorry he was, and she had a healing cry in his arms.

It isn't only the big secrets that we're afraid to tell. Many of us are uncomfortable saying anything that might be construed as even slightly confrontational: "I don't want to go to the Taj Mahal Cafe. I want to go to the Bean Sprout Club for dinner." "I'm sad that we didn't make love last night." "Thursday's my birthday and I hope you'll remember because I'll be terribly disappointed if you don't." But of course it's precisely the things you're afraid of telling your sweetheart that will show him or her who you really are.

Here's how to be emotionally brave: Whenever you're having the slightly unsettled feeling that comes from not saying what's on your mind, try asking yourself: What is it that I'm *not* saying? (Usually the words you're afraid to say are right there in your mind like in one of those little cartoon balloons.) Then ask yourself: Why am I not saying it right *now?* Maybe there's a good reason the kids are crying, you have to walk out the door in five minutes for a business meeting, your mother's on the phone—and you probably should hold your comments for later. But if there isn't a good, practical reason for not speaking *now,* just open your mouth and spit out the words that are dying to get out. You'll feel better—and your relationship will also get better as it holds more of the truth of who you and your sweetheart really are. ☯

REVEAL WHAT MAKES
YOU FEEL LOVED

*K*irsten fell in love with Tommy because on the first date he showed up at her house wearing a red and black checked flannel shirt, carrying two bottles of German beer, a box of crackers, and a wedge of Limburger cheese. "It was great," she said. "He believed me when I told him I loved Limburger cheese."

Meg, her best friend, wasn't impressed. "If somebody showed up to court me with Limburger cheese," she said, "I might not be insulted but I certainly wouldn't be happy. Give me a bouquet of pink carnations any day."

As the difference between Meg and Kristen demonstrates, love doesn't have its effect if it doesn't come in the form we need, no matter how much the person who loves us is trying. And all too many of us are sitting around waiting for, or worse yet, expecting that our darlings will automatically know precisely what makes us feel loved, and exactly when, where, how, and in what form to deliver it to us.

This is what I call "The Limburger Cheese Theory of Love." It states quite simply that everybody has his or her own particular ordinary (or extraordinary) preferences, and that nobody's going to make you feel loved if you don't tell him or her exactly what your preferences are. If Limburger cheese is what makes you feel loved, then you'd better tell your mate to give you Limburger cheese.

Whether we know it or not, we all have a secret laundry list of what makes us feel loved: his carrying your photo in his wallet; her scratching the back of your head; his cooking dinner for you; her wearing your favorite blue tee-shirt to the gym. What's on your list? Think about it, write it down, and share it with your partner.

Of course you'll never be loved exactly, entirely, always, or precisely in all the ways you want. But give your sweetheart a chance to make you feel as loved as possible by telling or showing him or her the items on your list.

Although people often say to me, "If I have to tell him or her, then it doesn't count." The truth is that nobody can guess the myriad little doo-dahs on your particular list. Love laundry lists are as different as our noses, and if you wait for the other person to figure what makes you feel loved, you could live your whole life without getting what you want. Getting the things on your list really does make you feel loved, even if you have to nail the list up on the bathroom wall or publish it in the Sunday *Times*.

So give your sweetheart a chance to really love you. Make your love laundry list. ☙

GO EASY ON YOURSELF

All of us know what a morbidly delicious temptation it can be to beat yourself up about almost anything that goes wrong in your relationship or, for that matter, in life in general.

If you have a fight or if you're too chicken to pick a fight, if you have an orgasm or if you don't, if it takes you forever to decide something or you decide impulsively, if you waste money or are a miser, if you're a neatness fanatic or a slob—whatever your habits, predilections, attitudes, or expectations, you find yourself blaming yourself for whatever goes awry in your relationship.

Rob blamed himself for years because whenever he and Jane had to make a decision about anything really important, he mulled it over for weeks. He analyzed it, slept on it, consulted with his, as he called them, "secret agents." Then, long after Jane had made up her mind and was, as it were, tap-tapping her pencil on the kitchen table in impatience, he'd finally make his decision.

Once his "stewing," as Jane referred to it, meant that they lost their chance to buy what they both had thought was their dream house. Rob was so busy analyzing the comparables and checking out loans, that three weeks into his process somebody else snapped up the house. Although Jane was disappointed, she actually recovered fairly quickly. "These things happen," she said. "Don't worry, we'll find another perfect house."

But long after they'd moved into a wonderful house, Rob was still beating himself up about the house his indecisiveness had lost. "I should have listened to Jane. I shouldn't be so perfectionistic about every single decision. I'm just a fuddy-duddy. Why can't I ever just make up my mind?"

The reality is that no matter what your style, no matter what you do precipitously or fail to do in time or in the right way, you're doing the best you can. Beating yourself up, blaming yourself, focusing endlessly on your faults—the way you might have been or should have been, done it or not done it—never improves the situation.

Look at yourself with compassion. Enjoy your curious little idiosyncrasies. Acknowledge that it's just fine to be you. Let it be all right that you're different from everybody else. Like the old Yiddish adage says, "If I be like him, then who will be like me?"

Being easy on yourself means that you accept yourself as you are, that you forgive yourself for your mistakes and go on, lovingly acknowledging your foibles, your idiosyncratic style. Only by being gentle with yourself can you also be good-natured and forgiving with the person you love. So give yourself a break; decide that you're just fine exactly as you are. ☙

CELEBRATE
THE EXCEPTIONAL

We all fall in love for a reason. There is something so unique and rare in the person you love that no matter what his flaws or her shortcomings, you return again and again in your mind to that ineffable quality which, for you anyway, is the essence of why you fell in love in the first place.

Taking note of that quality, remarking on it to your beloved, talking about it to your friends and children, will help keep your love fresh and vivid. We all enjoy hearing how wonderful we are: "You're so organized. I'd never even make it to the office with my briefcase if it weren't for you." "You are always so calm. Without your level head I'd probably be in the loony-bin by now." "You always know just the right thing to say to make me feel better."

Compliments are the verbal nourishment of the soul. They generate self-esteem and in a very subtle way create a person in the full spectrum of his or her essence. Compliments invite the person who is complimented to embrace a new perception of him- or herself. Just as layers and layers of nacre form a pearl over an irritating grain of sand, so compliments collect around us, developing us in all our beauty.

Celebrating the exceptional will make you aware not only of the value of the other person but also of your own specialness. To contemplate the uniqueness of your mate is, at the same time, to inform yourself about your own fine qualities. For the exceptionalness of your beloved is a reflection of you; you would not be in the arms of this incredible person if there weren't also something very special about you. To honor your wife's beauty is to be reminded of your own worthiness. To relish your husband's sensitivity is to be made aware that you are the kind of person in whose presence such emotional elegance can flourish.

In such ways do we confirm that we are not only lucky in love but worthy of being loved. To see the appropriateness of your being together is to have a sense of hope and joy about your mutual love. Therefore, lavish praise on the person you love, and the blessings will come back to you a thousandfold. ♥

PRAISE THE ORDINARY

 *L*ife as we know it, unfortunately, includes a multitude of things that are boring, tedious, and at times downright offensive. Cleaning up after the dog mess, playing Chutes and Ladders with your three-year-old son for the thirtieth time that day, having to cook dinner at eight o'clock after an exhausting day at the office—none of these are the things that give life its special joy.

The fact that as a part of loving one another we do, and continue to do, these ordinary and sometimes spirit-crunching things is a testament to the good-natured generosity of love. It is also a measure of the lengths to which love is willing to go in order to show its human kindness.

Praising these ordinary acts—"You did a great job on the dinner for my boss," "Thanks, honey, for cleaning out the closet," "It means so much to me that you always have milk in the house for my coffee," "I appreciate your always paying the bills"—can make doing the ordinary bearable. As my friend Kim the caterer says, "It's nice to be acknowledged for even the smallest of virtues."

When we get praised for such things, not only are we given the sense that the prosaic things we do are appreciated, but also that our partner knows we do them out of love. In marriage, it's easy to dwindle into a maid or a handyman, to feel as if your only connection to one another is through doing the domestic chores. But when you praise these ordinary undertakings, you acknowledge that, although they are not the highest calling you can both aspire to, they are, nevertheless, little ordinary acts of love.

Praise can make your beloved feel grateful for the opportunity to do the pedestrian and sometimes even wretched little tasks of life. That's because when you articulate how much you value your sweetheart for doing these simple things, you keep the pedestrian in its place. By so doing, you can also remember that you love one another for higher, deeper, and far more special reasons. ☙

BE A PERSON OF
YOUR WORD

*W*ords—and the way our actions do or don't stand behind their meaning—have an incredible capacity to wound us or to heal us. In a very real sense, words create reality. We all invest one another's words with our own hopes, fears, and expectations. Therefore, to keep your love alive, be a person of your word.

Being a person of your word creates faith in a relationship. It means not only that you will keep your promises, but in a more general sense, that you will say what you intend and then do what you say.

Nothing can erode a relationship as consistently or as deeply as too many words that mean nothing. For many of us, the biggest betrayals in our lives were delivered in the form of words that weren't true: "He said he was working late at the office, but all that time, he was having an affair." "My father promised to take me to Europe, but then he married my stepmother and went with her instead." "She swore he was just a friend, but come to find out, she'd been in love with him for years."

Since we've all been wounded by words, when we encounter unkept promises, we can very quickly be shaken to the core. We'd like to believe that we can expect endless emotional resilience from our partners, that it's acceptable time and time again to not quite say what we mean or say something that turns out not to be true, but in reality, our hearts can only stand so many little white lies or unintentionally broken promises. At some point, our faith begins to erode, and we start taking note of the number of times our mate didn't do what he or she said. In a very subtle way, we begin to discount his or her words. Without even noticing it, we begin not to listen, not to trust even the things our partner may still really mean.

So, aside from exceptions that are unavoidable— you promised to go to his college reunion, and your back gave out the night before; you'd said you'd meet him at seven, but the car had a flat—make every effort to mean and do what you say. Being a person of your word will build a fortress of trust in your relationship, and that trust will allow you to truly savor the words of love and praise that are the hallmark of an abiding love. ☺

CRITICIZE IN PRIVATE

*W*e all do things that are less than perfect—some of us talk too fast or interrupt constantly; others are perpetually late, sloppy about housekeeping, or overly perfectionist in our work habits. The things we do wrong are enough of an embarrassment to us that we certainly don't need to be reminded about them in public.

Registering such seemingly innocent or small-time complaints as "You never remember to take out the garbage," or "You always spill on your new clothes," even jokingly in the presence of friends, dinner guests, the plumber, your aunt, or a mother-in-law, is degrading to another person's essence. It has the effect of making him or her feel small, worthless, and punished in the presence of people among whom he or she would like to feel whole, effective, and worthy.

It doesn't do much to solidify your relationship either. How much would you feel like helping your wife take the car to the garage if, when you show up at her office, she says in front of her boss that she can't believe how long it took you to get here?

Reprimands always have a painful reference to childhood. They harken us back to a haunting sense of inadequacy, the feeling of powerlessness we sometimes had when we were small and at the mercy of our parents. For this reason, it is doubly painful to be reminded of our flaws, shortcomings, and failures in front of anyone except our intimate dear ones, whom we may legitimately hope will try to understand and forgive.

It's true that we all have disturbing little inadequacies that bear remarking on; when they're noted in private, we can be inspired to change. Indeed criticism, like encouragement, can shape the direction of our path and, therefore, serves a wonderfully creative function.

But when criticism is leveled in public, it diminishes our dignity, and far from correcting whatever needs to be improved, makes us skittish and afraid. We begin to feel that we're not acceptable as ourselves and eventually, in order to even up the situation, we may begin to withdraw our acceptance from our partner, until the public persona of our relationship is a catty downward spiral of teasing, judgments, and put-downs.

Public maligning is the antithesis of loving support and closeness. Rather than being an invitation to change, reprimanding is a spirit-breaking act. Preserve your love by graciously keeping silent about the things you'd like to correct until you're in the privacy of one another's arms. ✆

DO THE UNEXPECTED

*S*arah surprised her husband, Matt, by appearing at his office on his birthday in black net stockings, top hat, and tails, carrying a cake, and singing "Happy Birthday." Jim told Abby he had to pick up some film for his new camera and asked if she'd come along for the ride. Then he drove to the park, unloaded a picnic basket from the backseat of the car, presented her with a gorgeous bouquet of red roses and, under the spreading elm trees, asked her to marry him.

Susie sometimes puts orange blossoms in Fred's bathwater; Fred serenades Susie from their bedroom balcony. Shelly tucks love notes into Bill's folded tee-shirts; Bill buys Shelly new nightgowns "for absolutely no reason."

Everybody (well, almost everybody) likes a surprise, the uninvited appearance of the utterly unexpected, the rabbit that comes out of the hat, the hidden treasure, the silver lining. The unanticipated leaves us happily off-kilter, so spice up your life by doing something completely different. Throw gardenia petals on the bed, put a love note in the freezer, read each other a bedtime story, bury tickets to the circus under the pillow, take your honey to a fortune-teller, follow your sweetheart around for a whole day with a camera and make a photo essay of her life, leave a erotic message on his answering machine, call her at work just to tell her you love her, serve a candlelight dinner in bed. Pretend you're asleep and then wake your spouse up to make love.

Doing the unexpected has a number of beautiful effects. It gives you an opportunity to enjoy your own imagination and utilize your (perhaps neglected) creativity; it makes your partner feel special and it enlivens your love.

It's easy to get in a rut. You can do the same old thing any time. It's the exceptional that makes love feel like love and not just a two-person version of the drab, dull, daily routine. So do the unexpected—whatever it is and as often as you can—and watch as your love turns from dishwater dull to the sparkle of champagne. 🕊

SHOWER EACH OTHER
WITH KISSES

A relationship needs to be S.W.A.K. Remember writing that on the back of a letter? It meant that the letter you sent, the words you wrote, and the feelings you had were all the more special because you sealed them with a kiss. Even when courtship is over, your love needs to be sealed and affirmed with a multitude of kisses. For kisses, the loving embrace of the lips, are the sign, more than almost anything else, that we like, love, cherish, and adore the person we are kissing.

Kisses, like those little candy hearts on Valentine's Day, can carry all our little (and big and magnificent) messages of love. They are the sweetest, simplest, common-denominator expression of love; whenever you give them, you are nurturing your bond.

Kisses have a multitude of meanings. They can be the sign that a romance is beginning; they can be the glue of affection or the counterpoint to passion. Wordless, they can speak anything from "Honey, I'm home," to "Congratulations," to "Darling, I adore you," to "I'm wild about you; you're the one I desire," to, at the other end of the spectrum, a simple, "I'm sorry."

As kisses are the portal to erotic life in new romance, so they are the life support system of erotic passion in a long-time love. They are the signature of passionate contact, the way we tell one another that we love and that we'd like to make love. But kisses aren't just the key-card to erotic passion. Once having entered the realm of sexual intimacy, they have a power and a beauty of their own. They sweeten and deepen the sexual encounter, make it more playful or tender, more full of feeling.

Kisses are the food of love. They make us feel ... kissed. Chosen, desirable, powerful, beautiful, sensual, joyful, happy, carefree, invincible, *loved*. Kisses lift the level of our experience from the daily and banal to the delicious and extraordinary. Kisses capture our attention and express our best intentions. So never underestimate the power of a kiss. ✌

SAY THE LOVE WORDS

*E*verybody wants to hear how much, and precisely why, he or she is loved. Even when we've been chosen, even when we've tied the knot, we still need the verbal reassurance that we are loved.

We need to be endeared, to feel that we are special, delightful, delicious, precious, irreplaceable to the one we love. We want to be singled out, to be told we are loved above all by the person who has chosen us.

We often think that having a feeling about someone is as good as saying it, but it isn't. Make no mistake—words mean a lot to all of us. We all walk around with a huge collection of insecurities, and none of us is so sure, so cut and dried in our conviction about our own self-worth that we don't need the inspiration of being told every which way, over and over again, exactly why, how, and how much we are loved.

We need to be *told,* and the words have to be heartfelt. There's just no comparison between the abstract "Of course I love you" and the direct "I love you," no contest between silence and "You're the light of my life; I want to be with you forever."

Even though some people may think it is corny, in the delicate layers of even the coolest of cucumber hearts is a lover who yearns to be adored. There's a hidden romantic in each of us, the person who fell in love, who was tantalized by music and moonlight, who waited breathlessly to hear the words that heralded new love: "I adore you. I can't live without you." And once wasn't—and never will be—enough. For even if we could we don't want to have to keep the faith about love. We want our hearts to be filled by hearing the love words over and over again.

So call your beloved by a special name and tell her often what delights you about her, why you so deeply love him. Say the mushy/gushy things you think people only say in the movies—and the more romantic, the more erotic, the more delicious, the better: "You're the woman of my dreams." "I love you to pieces." "You're my angel." "You're a wonderful man." "You're a fabulous lover."

Love words are a tonic for love, an elixir for passion, a medicinal balm for fading romance. Life is infested with ordinariness, and there isn't any reason why love should be too. Love is what we fall into in order to partake of magic; love is how we fly. Words are the wings of romance, the way in which, more than any other, we elevate ourselves above the ordinary and pedestrian. Nothing can sustain the high pitch of romance better than beautiful love words, generously and endlessly spoken. ☯

ASK IF YOU CAN HELP

*W*e are all sufficiently occupied with the things we do for ourselves and the things we have no choice about doing for our jobs, spouses, and/or children that we don't necessarily have the time or inclination to do anything additional. Without helping anyone else, we have more than enough to keep us busy. That's why offering to help is a form of emotional graciousness that can add a lovely patina to your relationship.

Offering to help is more than just being willing to divide up the burden of the chores. It is a way of saying that, for no reason other than love, you are willing to enter into your sweetheart's undertakings. "Honey, I see you've been up all night doing the taxes; is there any way I can help you this morning?" "Do you need a hand with the groceries?" "Your cold's getting worse; would you like me to get you some cough medicine?" "You sound really blue; would you like to talk about it?" Help can come in many forms. It can be verbal solace (telling your honey everything's going to be all right), physical deliverance (lending a hand with the dishes), emotional comfort (listening to your sweetheart's woes), and a jack-of-all-trades willingness to do whatever is needed ("Is there anything I can do for you?").

Offering to help says that we want our beloved's life to be comfortable and gracious, and we're willing to expend some energy to make it so. More than that, by offering to help, we acknowledge we that we're not living in a vacuum, that we're not just born into the world to sit around and be waited on like Old King Cole. The world is not our oyster; our sweetheart is not our slave.

Offering to help is also an act of loving awareness. It says that, minute by minute, we specifically notice what's going on with the person we love and that we are willing to participate in his or her circumstances even at a very mundane level. This endears you to your love because, in a multitude of tiny, subliminal ways, he knows you're paying attention, she knows that you care. It's another way of affirming your connection, of saying you see yourself not as an island, but as part of the mainland created by your love. ☺

LISTEN FOR THE MESSAGE
UNDER THE WORDS

*R*ecently, at a party, a dear friend of mine walked in quite late. When I went over to give her a hug a few minutes later, I could feel that she didn't really receive it. Instead of responding, she started talking in an offhanded way about being late—she'd had to visit her brother, who was in the hospital; there was a traffic jam; it was raining. "Where are the hors d'oeurves?" she finally asked. "I'm starving." About then, I put my hand on her arm, looked her straight in the eye and said, "Sarah, you don't have to be so brave." Leaning her head on my shoulder, she said, "I'm so scared he's not going to make it," and then she started bawling like a child.

What we say is often not what we mean. Our true feelings are frequently hidden in the intricate secret spaces between the words we utter. Most of us don't have the language to put the full extent of our feelings into words, and lots of times we're not even sure what we're feeling anyway. For most of us, expressing our feelings precisely—especially when what we're feeling is sorrow, vulnerability, or shame—is extremely difficult. In the presence of such emotions, our words are often pitifully inaccurate, and what we reveal with our eyes and bodies is a much truer representation of our real message.

Therefore, when love listens, it listens with an ear

and a heart to the unspoken. When you listen to your sweetheart, attend also to what he or she isn't saying in words. Reach for the meanings that are being expressed through the twitching finger, the heaving chest, the furrowed brow, the tear-clouded eye.

When you listen for the message under the words, you are listening with a feeling consciousness. From this place you can try to reach in with words of your own to touch the depths of the other person. Perhaps you can ask a very tender question: "You say you're happy, but your eyes look sad. Would you like to tell me about it?" An open, inviting question can make your loved one feel safe enough to talk, and as your conversation moves delicately forward, the two of you can open the ground to a much deeper knowing, the knowing that comes from having heard the unspoken. ☙

WALK A MILE IN
YOUR SWEETHEART'S SHOES

*O*ne of the great pitfalls in any relationship is to use the other person as the handy-dandy dartboard for all the things that are irritating you. You can easily fall into the habit of blaming him for everything that goes wrong, and/or expecting her to make everything right.

In order to avoid succumbing to this unkind possibility, try walking a mile in your sweetheart's shoes. Walking a mile in your sweetheart's shoes means that you will put yourself in her place, allow his experience to penetrate your consciousness, and feel it deeply enough so that you can console one another if necessary and not blame each other if tempted.

So, anytime you're sure he or she is at fault for your bad mood, the broken computer, the leak in the roof, or the fact that life is boring, try putting yourself in his or her place. Imagine that you are she and bring to mind the myriad stresses, insults, assaults, disappointments, and disasters, miniscule and gigantic, that are currently besetting her life. Take a minute to think about the traumas your partner may be going through right now.

If you have trouble identifying with what your partner is feeling, if his boots are too big or her glass slipper only has room for your big toe, here's an exercise to try: Become your sweetheart. Begin by saying,

"I am ..." and call yourself by your sweetheart's name. Then, pretending you are he or she, start talking about what's going with "you." What's upsetting or delighting you right now? What has bruised or dampened your spirits? Try to see from inside his or her consciousness how your own critical, unsupportive, or blaming behavior feels when you are the person who has to receive it. What do you wish the person who loves you could do to understand or console you?

This is a very useful and often deeply moving exercise, especially when the two of you are at an emotional impasse. It's an opportunity for learning empathy from the inside by experiencing your own behavior through the other person's consciousness as you assume for a moment his or her emotional identity. "Being" her or him can move you very readily to a point of compassion that inevitably clears the way for more understanding between you.

Walking a mile in your sweetheart's shoes will enable you to see around the corner of your own assumptions, to discover that in our need to be loved and understood, we are all one. ☻

SAY "THANK YOU"

Whatever is given to you, in whatever form it comes—praise, cash, kisses, compliments, candy, time, listening, lovemaking, letters, a new hat, a new house, a new car, a new baby, a planned vacation, a surprise vacation, an insight, a sense of security, a bouquet, the sharing of some feeling—say "Thank you." Saying "Thank you" has a great effect on both partners. For the person being thanked, a "thank you" is a mirror of the love he or she has given. It not only increases our sense of ourselves as loving persons but enlarges our capacity to be loving. Of course we don't give something just to get thanked, but getting thanked allows us to see the value of what we have been given and makes us willing to give again.

Saying "Thank you" is also important for the person who says it. On the simplest level, it's an act of courtesy, a recognition of the good thing the other person has done. But on a much deeper level, it's a way of changing our consciousness about the nature of our relationships. For, in uttering our gratitude, we anchor in our minds the fact that we've been given to and are cherished.

It's all too easy, in any relationship, to become (internally, at least) a whining, complaining grump who feels as if the other person has never done, and will never do, anything nice or special for you. Saying "Thank you" dispels this feeling of hopelessness and creates an internal attitude of optimism. A pathway is formed in our minds that in time becomes a thoroughfare; the belief that we have been treated with generosity and goodness of heart, that we have, if you will, been loved, begins to take root in our consciousness. In this sense, saying "Thank you" is a character-building act. It develops a positive view of the person we love and also of the world.

Just as millions of snowflakes pile up to create a blanket of snow, the "thank you's" we say pile up and fall gently upon one another until, in our hearts and minds, we are adrift in gratitude. ✆

Treasuring Your Relationship

Your relationship is a precious jewel.
Not everyone has been given such a gift.
Treasure it, hold it in your hand and up to
the light,
and let its extraordinary beauty open your
heart
and transform your life.

PAY ATTENTION TO
THE TIMING

*T*iming is the mystical component of any relationship that refers to when things happen. It's the perfect moment, the magical conjunction of events, the folding together of one person's movement through time with another's—in perfect harmony.

Relationships themselves, and every event, behavior, and action within them, have their own unique and perfect timing. Just as the ideal mate often shows up only when you've completely given up on ever falling in love, so it is that within the sacred walls of a relationship there are perfect moments for everything, a choreography of timing that can either support or detract from the grace of your relationship.

Timing is a sensitive reflection of the myriad things about us: our histories ("I can't stand to do the dishes right after dinner because my mother was so compulsive that she'd start washing the dishes before we even finished dessert"); our metabolisms ("I'm just not a morning person"); our methods of apprehending reality ("I'll never get it if you talk about it for an hour; tell me what you need, let me go for a walk, and I'll be able to give you an answer when I get back"); our emotional sensitivities ("I just can't handle more than one complaint at a time; my father used to sit me down on Saturday night and read me a list of all my mistakes for the week"); and our personal quirks ("I don't know why—I just wake up at four in the morning").

Sensitivity to timing is awareness of the propitious moment, span of time, or appropriate circumstance for any given happening. It is the intuitive awareness that there is such a thing as the perfect moment—to say the word, to initiate the sexual encounter, to offer the gift, to express a complaint. Being sensitive to timing in relationship means that you will be conscious, first of all, of your own needs about the appropriation of time—for privacy, for being together, for handling conflict, for making love, for doing your share of the chores. It means also that you will communicate your needs and preferences and be aware that your partner's rhythms may be entirely different from yours. Timing, just like who pays what share of the bills, is something you must negotiate.

Sensitivity about timing adds grace to any union. If, together, you don't cultivate this sensitivity, you'll be continually jamming up against the differences in your time frames, saying the emotionally loaded thing at an inauspicious moment, or generally feeling abused in the realm of time. Conversely, when you learn to choose the perfect moment—to say the heart-touching words, to present the sapphire ring—you'll turn your relationship into a beautifully choreographed performance of the exquisite dance of your love.☙

PUT YOUR LOVE
ON A BILLBOARD

*P*amela and Don, who'd been married for years, were out to dinner with some of Don's business associates, including a couple of newlyweds. In congratulating them on their marriage, Don said, "I'm so happy for the two of you because marriage has been so wonderful for me. Pam's so intelligent and beautiful and witty. She believes in me when I try; she comforts me when I fail; I always know that she loves me—and she gets my jokes. That's why she's the perfect woman for me."

"That means more to me than all the things you've ever said in private," Pamela said when he'd finished. Don's remarks became a bouquet of compliments for Pam, a celebration of their marriage, and an inspiration for their tablemates.

Putting your love on a billboard, like Don did, is the opposite of acting as if your relationship should be one of the best-kept secrets in the Western world. Instead of hiding it under a bushel, you hold it up like a banner for everyone to see.

We sometimes think that keeping a lid on our love is the socially correct thing to do. It's as if we've signed a contract that says, "In private we love; in public we act like civilized strangers." The truth is, nothing makes us feel better than to be lauded in public or to experience in company the fact that our mate thinks our relationship is worth crowing about. It's as if by seeing our relationship or spouse through the eyes of others, we're allowed to discover from a slightly different perspective what a wonderful treasure it is.

I'm not talking here about making a passionate public spectacle of your romance; simply about honoring it publicly, letting the people who form the social fabric of your life know that your love is precious to you, that it fills your heart, and gives meaning to your life.

Putting your love on a billboard goes beyond the perfunctory "I'd like to thank my lovely wife," or "Without the continued support of my husband" and reaches into the realm of deeply felt and highly specific acknowledgement. It gives the partner you are celebrating a deliciously puffed-up thrill to be so celebrated and gives the people who hear your testimonial a sense of hope about the power of love. ☙

NEGOTIATE
THE MUNDANE

*T*he trouble with life is that it's so daily. Sooner or later, every relationship comes down to who's going to take out the trash. Facing that any relationship includes what at times can feel like a seemingly endless amount of chores is one of the higher duties of love. For it acknowledges that love, an experience of transcendence, occurs in the mundane, material world. Accepting this is in itself an act of love, because it means that for the cause of love we will humble ourselves to do all manner of boring and annoying tasks graciously.

One of the dangers of the daily nature of life is that we may be inclined to see these chores as being a consequence of our relationships and not of life itself. It's a great temptation to blame the other person for the ickiness of ordinary life, as if were we still living alone we wouldn't have to make the bed, do laundry, deal with the exploding water heater, or fix the ailing car. It's also easy to get unreasonable and picky about neglected tasks or our partner's chores we sometimes end up doing. However, our responsibility in love is not to expect that such trivial responsibilities will disappear or to assume that just for love the other person (or we ourselves) will, without batting an eye, just do everything.

Rather, real love knows that the dishes need to be

done and is willing to negotiate about it. True love is grateful that the burden can be shared. This means talking about it, figuring out who's going to do what, making a list, and not expecting that some elves will come along and do it all. Negotiation also requires compromise—for example, accepting, without complaint, that the other person might not clean the toilet bowl as perfectly as you would or being willing to do certain tasks, like washing his filthy work jeans, that you wouldn't have to do if you were living alone.

Negotiating the mundane means that you accept the dishpans and trashcans of life and decide together how chores are going to be done. Then, instead of being bones of contention and the most significant things in your life, chores can recede into the background so you can do the really important things— like discovering your destiny and making love. ⊛

ACKNOWLEDGE THE
HARDSHIPS YOUR
CIRCUMSTANCES CREATE

*J*ust being ourselves creates burdens for our loved ones. No matter who we are—a movie star, a mother of five who's married for the second time, a graduate student, a diabetic, or someone with an upside-down work schedule—we've all arrived at our relationships dragging along the barnacles of circumstances that, at times, make us difficult to love. Stepchildren, ailing parents, broken cars, wacky sisters—we all have conditions that make loving us a hardship for the person who has chosen to love us.

The sad truth is that most of us have too many obligations and too little time. We don't mean to drive our spouses crazy by having to attend ten late-night meetings in a row, by having twenty outfits strewn across the bedroom floor because we haven't had time to pick them up, by having a toothache six days running—but we do. In these and myriad other ways, we unintentionally abuse each other. We all require too much from each other; in a sense, we're all asking one another to do the impossible all the time.

Love makes our partners willing to put up with all this real-life nonsense, but the truth is we need to be mindful of, grateful for, and apologetic about the hardships that our circumstances cause. It's easy to react from defensiveness or guilt by thinking or saying, "Putting up with my sick mother can't be all that bad," or "He shouldn't complain about how much I have to work."

But we really do need to own up to all these things. Remembering how we stretch one another and saying the appropriate "Please bear with me," "Thank you for putting up with my insane schedule," or simply "I'm sorry" will create, in the midst of these taxing situations, moments in which we can appreciate the inordinate generosity and forbearance of one another. Rather than becoming irritants that are divisive and destructive, our hardships can then become occasions for deepening intimacy. Acknowledging what we inflict and require makes it possible for our mates to endure the unendurable and can forge a new and stronger connection of love between us. ☙

KEEP IN TOUCH

*I*n these days of inordinately busy and complex schedules, it is actually possible to lose touch with the person you love, sometimes for days at a time. That's why we need to make an effort to keep a hand on not only the pulse of our obligations and plans but also on the heartbeat of our intimate relationships.

Keeping in touch means that you will keep your partner thoughtfully apprised of your life and times—your schedule and obligations as well as variations in routines and plans. There's nothing worse, for example, than having a sick child and being unable to track down your mate. Or being told he'll arrive at six that evening, only to have him show up two hours later. Or setting aside a weekend to be together only to be informed at the last minute that she can only spare from two to four Sunday afternoon. Of course, emergencies and exceptions come up, but having the commitment to fill one another in as much as possible, as soon as possible, will give your honey the resilience to withstand the irritating exceptions.

But keeping in touch should be more than merely an exchange of scheduling information. It also means that you'll find ways to communicate your love on a regular basis, regardless of how busy you are. In this way, you keep telling your sweetheart that it's him you want to come home to, that it's her you adore.

One couple I know keeps a book on the living room table. When either of them has to be gone, he or she never goes away without leaving a message of love for the other person. They've been married eight years and the book is the heartfelt tracing of a daily life lived out in thoughtfulness and love.

Ellen, who travels a lot for business, never goes out of town without leaving a love note for her husband, John, propped up on his pillow. And he never welcomes her home from one of these jaunts without having arranged a bouquet of flowers for her by the bed.

Michelle has a spot on the back doorjamb where she leaves a welcome home note for Paul, her sweetheart. And Sam, whose work takes him out of the country for weeks at a time, sends a postcard home every day. It always says the same thing: "I would be having a wonderful time —if only you were here." Another man, a busy attorney, calls home every day to say, "Have I told you today that I love you?" These seemingly little gestures can make all the difference to our hearts in an obligation-hobbled world.

Keeping in touch is the antidote to taking for granted. It means that you treat your lover as special; it's a way of reminding yourself that your love is special too. ✪

TAKE INTIMATE TIME

All too often we treat our relationships as if they were cars that could run without gasoline. We expect them to look good, keep us safe inside, give us a self-image, and get us where we are going—all without even the basic maintenance. Don't let your relationship run out of gas. Intimate time is the fuel of a fine relationship. Taking the time means that rather than expecting your relationship simply to provide you with all the benefits you want—sex, companionship, emotional solace, the parenting of your children, financial security—you understand that a relationship requires the sustenance of shared private thoughts and feelings, and you make a commitment to find the time for this sharing.

Intimate time can run the gamut from the "five-minute check-in" at a set time (the breakfast or dinner table, just before sleep) that covers the bases of information about your day, to a daily reunion of twenty minutes or more when you each have time to reveal yourself on a more intricate level. Here you can talk more thoroughly with one another, revealing your fears, your goals, your ongoing intentions and daily frustrations, your joys. This is when you can share your hurts and disappointments (both those you have caused each other and those inflicted by the outside world), encourage one another, and make plans.

Taking intimate time also means creating opportunities for the other sweet intimacies of love: a walk on the beach or around the block in the snow; a hideaway weekend in the desert, the mountains, or simply at the Motel 6 around the corner. It also means creating the chance to make love in a leisurely way, to spend a whole day in bed, to curl up together on the couch, kiss more than perfunctorily, hold hands across the dinner table.

Frankly, I believe if you can't find twenty or thirty minutes a day for some kind of intimate encounter, your relationship is a toboggan on a downhill run toward a big black rock. Taking intimate time for your love means that instead of depriving your relationship of the sweet essentials it needs, you will be generous in finding time for them. ✿

KINDLE THE ROMANCE

*R*omance is the champagne and frosted glasses of love, the magic that gives love a tango to dance to, a fragrance to remember, and a fantasy-come-true to hold in your heart. Romance is the anti-dote to ordinariness, the inspiration for passion; whenever you fold it into your relationship, you instantly elevate it to a more delicious state of being. Romanced, you feel beautiful or handsome; life becomes ripe with hope; the moon, stars, and planets bathe you in a cascade of beneficent light; and you believe that everything is possible—your sweetest, wildest, and most cherished dreams will certainly come true.

At least that's certainly how we feel in the rosy blush of new romance. But the feeling of romance doesn't just stick around all by itself. As time goes on, it takes effort, ingenuity, intuition, and sometimes even a willingness to feel foolish, to keep the moonlight magical. That's because somewhere along the line, without quite paying attention, we stop doing the things that kindled romance in the first place: we forget to bring the long-stemmed roses and to whisper the sweet nothings; we leave the lights on (or off), we trade in the black lingerie for flannel pajamas. In short, we start treating one another as roommates instead of passionate lovers.

But we can all still have romance in our lives, no

matter how long we've been together. Chill the glasses. Remember the roses. Install the new dimmer, light the candles, and forget about the wax drip-dripping on the table. Play the song you first heard on your honeymoon. Dress the bed in red sheets. Drive up the hill to watch the sunset and kiss (and kiss) in the car.

Every so often, Ian plays a romantic SOS trick on Sonja. He calls her up from somewhere, says he's having trouble with his car, and asks if she can please come pick him up. When she arrives, it turns out he's "stranded" near some hotel. He hands her a beautifully wrapped present—a dress or a sexy new nightgown. He checks them into a room and orders dinner from room service. After dinner, they go dancing and then make passionate love. Needless to say, Sonja is ecstatic every time.

When it comes to kindling romance, you have to be willing to be creative, even if at first you feel shy or embarrassed. Remember, you weren't embarrassed by all those love notes and love songs when you were falling in love. The art of romance takes practice. The more you allow yourself to stretch the limits of what feels comfortable to you, the more inventive you'll become, especially if your initial efforts garner a positive response. (And if you're the receiver of these endeavors to enchant, be sure to respond with appreciation. If you do you will definitely increase the romance quotient in your life.)

So whatever your particular romantic preferences may be, be sure to indulge them as much as you can. Don't let opportunities slip through the cracks. Like the relationship it will embellish, romance is a very special art form whose greatest reward is the joy of true passion. ☺

FIGHT THE GOOD FIGHT

No relationship is without conflict—differences of opinion, preference, and even direction—and a relationship is only as good as the conflict it can contain. By this I mean that a relationship has vitality only to the degree that it can endure the stresses of individual differences and resolve them through healthy conflict, so that the relationship and the individuals in it can move toward greater authenticity.

The notion of the totally tranquil, we-never-fight relationship as the paragon of love is a dangerous fallacy. All too often the persons in such a situation are scared to death of testing the resilience of their relationship by airing their real differences, or have so suppressed their individual selves that their differences seem invisible.

Many of us are scared of conflict because we don't know how to fight. We're afraid our own anger will run away with us, that we'll lose control and become vicious, vituperative, or even physically destructive. We're also afraid of the other person's anger—will he or she yell, throw things, slam the door, walk out? These behaviors can sometimes occur and can even be a real danger, especially for people who have been abused with anger themselves. But even they can learn to express anger in a constructive way.

The sign of a good fight is that it makes you both

feel you have discovered something, that you know one another better. Even if you fight again and again about the same issues (and most of us do), a good fight gives you hope about the future because you have gained a measure of insight about something that previously baffled or frustrated you.

Here's some help:

1. Try to see what you're angry about. This is usually something very specific: "That you didn't call," not "Because life is miserable."

2. State your feeling and why you feel that way: "I'm angry that you didn't call because it makes me feel unloved."

3. Say what you need in recompense: "I need you to apologize."

4. After your mate has given the apology, ask yourself and him or her if you feel totally resolved.

5. Kiss and make up.

For example, "I'm angry at you for yelling at me about burning the tea kettle. You embarrassed me in front of Kay. It made me feel belittled to have her hear you talk to me like that. I need you to apologize."

"I'm sorry, honey. I was in such a rush this morning and was anxious about that big meeting. I was out of line. I don't want to make you feel that way. Please forgive me."

This, of course, would win the Academy Award for

Most Civilized Fight, and with your high feelings and sense of frustration over the number of times the hateful thing has happened, to say nothing of your just plain humanness, you probably won't always be able to muster quite so much graciousness. In any case, try to remember:

1. A good fight isn't a free-for-all. Don't say everything you feel like saying even though you may have a legitimate gripe. Remember that words can wound, and after the fight you don't want a battered mate.

2. Be specific with your complaints. Don't throw in all your grievances since time began.

3. Let the other person's words sink in before you take up your cudgel. Remember, you're having this fight to learn something, to arrive at some new insight as well as an immediate resolution.

4. Go easy on yourself and your honey when you don't do it perfectly. ☺

FACE YOUR
DIFFICULTIES HEAD ON

*E*ven in the most successful and agreeable union, there are differences (some irreconcilable) and incompatibilities (some vast), which are the mysterious unresolvables upon which that relationship becomes a kind of meditation.

Most of the time, we live with these difficulties as a kind of wearying background noise to the interplay of our relationships. They haunt us as sorrows, frustrate us as unfulfilled needs, prickle our consciousness as irritating secrets and unexpressed resentments. How we handle—or don't handle—them has a great effect on our relationships. Keeping the difficulties to yourself (whether they be imperfections of your partner or of the relationship itself) won't make you feel any better, nor will it move you toward bridging the distance that your differences represent.

What does hold the possibility of creating change is facing your differences head on and lovingly talking about them—"Facing and Telling," as I call it. What this means is that you will dive into even that most risky of emotional waters—sharing with your partner the things that are irritating or disruptive.

This involves, first of all, being truthful with yourself about what these things are: "It really is totally unacceptable to me that he's started smoking again. It scares me; I feel like he's killing himself." "I wish she had a spiritual life; it's painful to me that we can't pray together."

Once you've faced the truth by yourself, hold on to it. Don't blurt it out; instead, write it down on a list. Then, with your partner, pick a time to talk about these things. You might want to do this regularly, once a week or once a month, just to keep the emotional slate clean or, if you prefer, choose a single, specific time when your secret "grudges" have mounted up.

The format, then, is to say very simply, "I need to tell you what's difficult for me right now." Then state, without anger or judgment, what's bothering you at the moment.

Your partner, the listener, should then respond by saying, "Thank you for telling me this; I'm sorry this is so difficult. I hope that in time, together, we can move beyond this problem."

In this ceremony, each partner takes a turn, both in revealing what's difficult and in responding. This isn't an exercise in making promises to change behavior. It is simply about revealing and acknowledging the difficulties, accepting that they exist, and believing that your relationship is strong enough to contain the truth of what you both reveal. When you've finished, conclude the process with a kiss and say "I love you" to each other. ֍

LEAVE THE KITCHEN SINK
IN THE KITCHEN

*W*hen you fight, leave the kitchen sink in the kitchen. What I mean by this is don't just gratuitously throw in things that don't belong in the current fight—every complaint you've had since the history of time began, something corroded and calcified from sixteen years ago, or the meanest, below-the-belt thing that you can possibly think of saying.

Kitchen-sink behavior isn't profitable. It doesn't do anything except fan the flames of contention and open an abyss of panic and pain your mate. Once you've gotten the satisfaction of watching the sink fly by and crash into the wall, you may have a hard time cleaning up after yourself.

So no matter what you're so furious about, try to resist the temptation to let it all hang out or to let the devil take the hindmost. It's important to stop and think before you let the other person have it. Ask yourself two questions:

1. Do I really need to say *this?* That is, does this horrible, angry, vituperative, or character-blasting thing really need to be said? Will it improve the immediate situation? Is there anything useful to be gained from saying, for example, that you not only think your sex life is awful now, but it has been for the past ten years? Will this or similar remarks speed up the other person's evolu-

tion, or your own, or is saying it just the indul-
gence of revved-up emotions that want release?

2. Do I really need to say this *now?* The diatribe you
want to indulge in may include some very valu-
able points that really do need to be expressed.
But is this the time to make them? Will you set
off a furor or engender a useful response?

Before you fire your verbal machine gun, it's
important to investigate the maturity of your emotional output. Just because you feel like saying something doesn't mean it has to be said in the way or at
exactly the moment that you feel like saying it.
Remember, your relationship is a precious thing that
deserves to be preserved. Look for a more appropriate
time and way to express your feelings so that your
relationship will be enhanced rather than eroded or
destroyed. 🌸

REMEMBER THE EARLY DAYS
OF YOUR LOVE

*I*n the bash and crash of daily life, it's very easy indeed to forget why we love one another: she's come home late for the sixth night in a row, he's been short-tempered and surly again, nobody's said anything sweet for what seems like ten weeks. It's at times like these that we need to remember the romantic days of falling in love.

In order to nourish and refresh your relationship, you need to remind yourself from time to time about the happy hours of your early love. Every love has the ravishing early moments of romance—the sunset walk along the pier, the tear-washed face of good-bye at the international airport, the stolen kisses when your love was still a secret. It's what you experienced in these moments that you need to remember and share.

"I saw her walking in the garden at the house where I was visiting, and her movements so totally enchanted me that I knew I had to marry her. I just wanted to be able to watch her forever."

"He asked me to go on a hike. We started up the mountain and I turned my ankle and started to fall. But instantly he caught me. 'Gotcha,' he said, and I fell back into his arms and felt totally protected. I could sense his great kindness and thought to myself, 'He's a wonderful man—I'm falling in love.'"

Just talking together about these memories can revive those wonderful feelings, especially if you do it in such a way that it brings you together, and not in a blaming "Remember-how-you-kissed-me-500-times-a-day-and-now-you-never-do" way. Whatever it was that made you fall in love, remembering it will give you the stamina and generosity of spirit to go on, a way to feel that, "Oh yes, there *is* a good reason to go through all the difficulties that we sometimes have."

Love that grows threadbare and dingy with time can be instantly revived by the memory of what was magic to both of you at the outset. Whatever bonded you initially was real and powerful, and you can lose sight of that as time goes on. When you allow yourself to remember your falling in love, you make the things that brought you together as strong as the things that are undermining your relationship at the moment.

So remember why you fell in love, and the magic will happen again. ☺

BE WILLING TO MAKE THE
GENEROUS GESTURE

*E*specially in fights where angry fevers are already running high, we all have a tendency to get stubborn, to bullishly hold our positions, and to be damned if we'll back down.

In any relationship longer than three weeks old there are probably grounds for divorce. One way or another we all do millions of things that bother, irritate, violate, and break the heart of one another. All isn't fair in love and war, and what I mean by this is that the abuses of both love and war are endless, and we'd better not try to delude ourselves into thinking otherwise.

It's because love has the capacity to infinitely wound us that, when we're in a tough spot with the person we love, we can feel as if we've gone miles beyond our limits and that, in order to preserve our dignity, our sanity, or our skin, we absolutely must not back down, give up, or give in.

Stubbornness does serve as self-preservation, and rightly so, for we shouldn't stand for the kind of mistreatment that is actually abuse. But it can also stand in the way of progress if we refuse to back down even when, for the sake of the union, we should. When we're feeling ripped off, taken advantage of, or ignored, impasses such as "I'm right," "No, I'm right"; "Be nice to me," "Not until you be nice to me first!";

"It's all your fault," "Whadda you mean? It's all *your* fault!" can send your relationship into a brutally plummeting downward spiral from which it may never recover.

A stalemate isn't a very creative place. Nothing can be accomplished, forgiven, resolved, or revised when we stand head to head refusing to budge. We can't expect progress unless one of the two billy goats butting heads takes the first step to unlocking horns.

Therefore, be willing to say, "OK, I'll back off and really try to listen to you this time." Or, for the really stubborn at heart, here's a trick: Say, "I'll be nice if you'll be nice," then, on the count of three, start talking again at the place where you were before you both got so stubborn.

True love flourishes in the air of compassion. The gesture that bridges the gap of abuse, exhaustion, and disappointment is the emotionally heroic act. Be willing to be a hero in your relationship by going beyond your limits to make the generous gesture, the gesture that will nourish and preserve your union. ☯

TIE UP YOUR EMOTIONAL
LOOSE ENDS

*E*motional loose ends are those little hanging-on, nagging incompletenesses between you and your mate: unexpressed resentments, unbandaged hurts, unresolved conflicts, unmentioned little embarrassments, requests that are hiding out in the background. Unsaid, they stand between you and your mate, spoiling your emotional bond, clouding the clarity you'd like to have with one another.

When you tie up emotional loose ends, instead of letting your conflicts, requests, and difficulties languish in the slough of non-expression, you bring them to a conclusion and make peace with one another before going on. Doing this implies that you both desire and believe you can bring your union to the place of emotional homeostasis, of calm, in which you can once again take the tender emotional risks that deepen a relationship.

A relationship needs a consistent, ground level of harmony, a safe place from which the people in it can take the chances that enhance their own growth and nurture the bonds that connect them. Tying up your emotional loose ends is a way of keeping this sanctuary clear.

We all have a tendency to let things go, to hope that whatever's amiss will just work itself out or disappear. Some things do become conveniently irrelevant in time, but the truth is that not resolving takes an incredible amount of energy. And all this energy could much better be used for kissing each other or making plans to go to the movies.

Yvonne was still mad at Claude about a fight they'd had on Friday. When they went out on Saturday night, instead of being able to relax and enjoy herself, she was cranky and unsettled. When Claude said, "I really hate it that you talk on the phone with Laura all the time," Yvonne was desvastated. She relied on the fun and support of her frequent chats with Laura, her best friend, and it was scary to think that Claude had such a negative reaction. But instead of telling him about it, Yvonne just "hoped he didn't really mean it," or that "he'd get over it." She even thought about making a snide remark about Ned, Claude's best friend, the next time they went golfing. But none of these efforts to shove things under the rug had worked. Laura was still upset, and not talking about it only had the effect of spoiling their Saturday night.

This is a perfect example of how emotional loose ends can turn into romantic nooses. So instead of building a gallows for your love, take the extra time and care to resolve your unfinished emotional business, no matter how trite or inconsequential it may seem. Love blossoms under blue skies and tying up emotional loose ends shoos all the dark clouds away. ☺

PLAY TOGETHER

*W*hen we play we feel the carefree joyfulness of our spirits. We are delivered from the bonds of obligation and responsibility to a sense of delight about ourselves. Playing allows us to rekindle the sense of the child in us, to go back to a time when life was new and full of possibility. Because inside we're all still young, we need to play as much as we can.

Playing alone or with others—a round of golf, an aerobics class, a soccer game, a tennis match—isn't just frivolous nonsense. Play creates balance. It's the safety net under the tightrope of modern life; it keeps us sane and functioning.

Playing alone is good. Playing together is better. Playing with the person you love is the premier form of play. Playing combines both the intrinsic joys of play with the opportunity to have a totally carefree experience with (and sometimes a mind-altering view of) the person you love. Seeing and being with him at his most spontaneous, at her most innocent and unguarded, can only deepen your appreciation of him, your sense of the specialness of her. For when we do what we love, we are most precisely ourselves.

Shared foolishness deepens bonds.

"Remember when we climbed the 500 steps up the sand dune and then when we got to the water tower it was all fenced in? We climbed up anyway and I ripped my shorts on the barbed wire fence. Wasn't that view incredible?"

"Remember when we held the croquet tournament over Labor Day and you won?"

"Remember when we went to the MacIntoshes' Halloween party and I was a ballerina and you were a cat?"

"Remember the summer we played badminton on the back lawn every night after supper?"

Playing together—whether you play house, play yard, play sports, play dress-up-and-go-out—always doubles the fun because you feel not only the pleasure of your sweetheart's company, but also the pleasure of the thing you love to do.

Therefore, *play play play.* Play well. Play hard. Play on. Play often. Play for keeps. ☺

CELEBRATE WITH
CEREMONIES

*L*ove flourishes when it's shored up by the joy of celebration. Celebrations acknowledge special events: birthdays, anniversaries, promotions, awards, graduations—the cycles of our lives and loves. Celebrations are the fairy dust that ritualistically enlivens the commonplace continuum of daily life. They keep us in touch with, and make us take note of, the things that make our lives and loves precious.

We were all delighted by ceremonies when we were children—the tooth fairy, the Christmas stocking, the Easter Bunny, the pony rides at birthday parties. Just because we've outgrown our childhood britches doesn't mean we've outgrown our need for ceremony. Even though we may have become more self-conscious we are still needy of such commemorative events in our lives.

It is these special moments, ritualized by their repetitiveness, that give us a sense of rootedness, that draw us close together. Indeed, it is the very fact that ceremony has a repetitive aspect that creates a certain portion of our enjoyment. We know that the magical things will unfold in exactly the same way as they have before and this in itself delights us.

Love needs the benediction of celebration and ceremony. Rick always gives Shelly a chocolate bunny for Easter. Suzanne and Ed always go back for their summer vacation to the cottage on the lake where Suzanne grew up. Mark and Marie always spend their anniversary at the hotel where one day, thirteen years ago, they first crossed eyes beside the pool.

Mary makes a nightshirt for Dennis every Christmas and embroiders its pocket with a coat of arms. Each year when the new shirt appears, Paul cuts out the old insignia from last year's shirt and keeps it in a special box where, by now, he has more than a dozen tokens of her love.

Walter always orders a bakery birthday cake for Cerise, one with stand-up numbers like the ones she had on her cakes when she was a little girl in France. He always writes the same thing on her card: "So you'll feel younger while you're growing older."

So celebrate the special occasions in your life with your own personal ceremonies. Ceremonies order and embroider our intimate lives. ✆

REVEAL YOUR FEARS

*W*hen you're in love, there aren't any extra points for being brave. Bravery is fakery, the antithesis of intimacy. Bravery is living a lie. In order to have a truly meaningful relationship, you need to be willing to talk about what you're afraid of.

For some reason, especially in the United States, we're all ashamed of being afraid. We're taught that fears are for sissies and that, when we finally "get it together," we will have transcended fear and can say, like Ernest Hemingway, that we're " 'fraid a' nothin.' "

The truth is that our fears refer to some very tender places in ourselves, areas where we've been hurt, where we haven't quite grown up, where we're not yet strong enough or have already had our fondest hopes smashed to bits. Our fears are as various as the petty fear of spiders or the fear of our own mortality. But no matter how inconsequential or overwhelming they may seem, they are reports from the fragile interiors of our psyches. In revealing them, we give our partners access to the points where we need to be nurtured; where, because of our vulnerabilities, we are most able to be loved.

Thus, unveiling your fears is an act of openness that counts on the loving response. It says, "I know you love me enough to allow me to show you my weakness. I trust you to be careful with me." When we tell our wives and lovers, husbands and sweethearts, that we're afraid, this trust in itself becomes a compliment to the beloved.

Disclosing your fears also brings you immediately to the level of greater intimacy, because one of our biggest fears is that everybody else has it all together and you alone are the only pathetic chickenhearted idiot on the face of the Earth. Interestingly enough, revealing what you are afraid of usually prompts the other person to divulge his or her fears too. In this way, exposing your fears puts you at once in alignment with the innermost self of the other person, with what he's afraid of, with where she feels terrified and alone. So reveal your fears, because it is being together in the midst of our vulnerabilities that is one of the most tender and touching experiences of being in love. ♥

SHARE YOUR DREAMS

*O*ur dreams, whether the dreams we have at night or the hopes and aspirations we have for our lives, represent some of the most profound, protected, and precious parts of ourselves. Because they are so private, when we share them we immediately create intimacy.

Images from our sleep are a map of our unsuspected and uncensored selves. They are messages to us and about us from the deepest reaches of our unconscious. In the enigmatic language of our own private symbols, they reveal the secrets we keep even from ourselves.

Telling your sweetheart your dreams is an act of self-revelation, for in opening the door to your unconscious in this way, you are allowing your spouse to meet you at a special and unguarded place, the place of magic that is often beyond common sense or even words. Whether or not your dreams make perfect sense to you or your partner (and you don't have to be Sigmund Freud to receive at least some of their meanings), being given a view of your beloved through this mysterious looking glass is to be taken into his or her spiritual privacy.

The same is true of the dreams that are our aspirations—for in revealing our hopes and longings, we are at once most exalted and most vulnerable. In speaking of what we desire, we also reveal how we can be disap-

pointed. The fact that you always wanted to be a ballerina (and can't even walk across the living room without banging into the wall) is something you don't
want everyone to know, but telling your sweetheart is
a way of opening up a sensitive part of yourself for
special nurturing.

None of us can live out all our dreams—life isn't
long enough. And we all have more talents than time
to explore them in. Although at some level we realize
that, as my mother used to say, "You can't do everything," there is also a sense of loss attached to letting
go of even our most ridiculous or offbeat dreams.
When we share our unfulfilled dreams, we are asking
our loved ones to meet us in a place of vulnerability,
where we can be apprehended not only for who we
are, but also for who we would like to have been.

Revealing your dreams is an act of trust. It means
you believe that the person who loves you desires to
see you in your secret essence without being horrified
or ashamed, without making fun of you. It means you
believe you can share your innermost secrets, and that
if your aspirations should turn to ashes, the person
you love will still be there to comfort you. ☙

TRUST ONE ANOTHER

*T*rue love is built upon trust, the emotional climate you jointly create as the atmosphere in which love can flourish. Trust is the sense that we are safe with one another, that in our moments of vulnerability, weakness, or great glory, we will not be betrayed.

To trust means that we start from the position of believing that our sweetheart is motivated by a deep concern for us, that he or she, in spite of occasional missteps or mistakes, truly has our well-being in mind. When we trust, we believe that the other loves us dearly and intends to love us well and long. Trust imagines the best; trust expects the happiest possible outcome. Trust serves with joy in the expectation that trust will be returned.

Trust develops trust. Acknowledging that you trust the person you love—with your life, with your heart, your body, your talents, your fears, your children, your worldly goods—invites him or her to become even more worthy of that trust. In a wonderful upward spiral, the compliment of trust encourages even more trustworthiness. Thus, the more you trust, the safer you become and the more you are able to love.

Just as trust engenders trust, doubt, its opposite, creates more suspicion. The more you suspect, expect, and imagine that your partner doesn't love you and doesn't want to care for you properly, the more it will become impossible for him or her to scale the wall of your doubt to give you the gift of love, the blessing of undying affection.

But trust comes from more than your own state of mind. It develops in response to the actions, words, and ways of the person you are choosing to trust. Trust is delicate, easily damaged; it can be destroyed by a single sentence of spirit-crushing attack, one thoughtless night of betrayal, a passel of lies. In matters of trust, we are the guardians of one another's psyches—and we must take the creation of trust as a serious responsibility.

Therefore, as well as trusting, be trustworthy yourself. Ask the best of yourself—for integrity with your actions, intentions, and words—so you may be a worthy partner in creating the atmosphere of trust that will be a lifetime cradle for your love. ☺

Taking Your Love to
a Deeper Level

Love is like a great tree.
It has a strong trunk and many branches.
If you climb to the top, you can see things
for miles around, things you never
imagined were there.

A great tree has deep roots,
the invisible structure that
keeps its whole growth in balance.
A love can be only as strong
as its deepest root reaches.

May your roots be long.

CONSOLE ONE ANOTHER

*M*ore, perhaps, than we would like to acknowledge, life is infused with tragedy. Everybody is given burdens of heart that are almost too much to bear; we all have sorrows and heartaches that bring us into landscapes of pain that at times seem untraversable. There are times when we feel that what we are experiencing will utterly devour or destroy us.

To be aware of this is to know how immense is the need for consolation. Faced with the magnitude of the tragic in our midst, we can do nothing but attempt to extend the healing gift even if we feel totally unequipped to offer it. For no matter how inadequate our unpracticed gestures may seem, they will surely reach into the place that is aching for solace.

Consolation is a spiritual undertaking. It begins with the state of grace that accepts we are all suffering and that it is one of our highest callings to enter into the vale of tears and abide there awhile with one another.

We all need to be willing to act as physicians of the spirit for one another during the painful times. For it is when we are assaulted by the visitation of life's sorrows that we most need to feel the presence of the person who loves us. It is when we are broken-hearted that we most need to be ministered to, when we are in grief that we need most to be taken into the arms of love.

Consoling is being willing to enter at the depth of the wound. To console is to join company with, to bond. It is to enter into another's sorrow and stand in its presence, to become witness to the unbearable so that, finally, it can be borne.

To console is to comfort—with your words, with your hands, with your heart, with your prayers. To console is to mourn with one another and thereby divide the power of the loss. In consoling you make yourself and the person you love less alone. You listen from the innermost place in yourself to the innermost place in her soul, respond from the most generous part of yourself to the neediest part of him. ☙

FORGIVE ONE ANOTHER

To forgive is to see the person who has offended you in an entirely different way, through the eyes of charity and love. This is a difficult but life-transforming task, for forgiveness breathes new life into a relationship and changes the chemistry between you from stale to breathtakingly sweet.

In a real sense, forgiveness begins with yourself, with the understanding that despite your best intentions, you too will fail, will find yourself doing the terrible things you thought only your enemies were capable of doing. To see yourself with compassion in spite of your failures is the beginning of forgiveness for others. For we can never take back into our hearts the person who has wounded us unless we can first be kind to ourselves about our own offenses.

Forgiveness requires emotional maturity and a willingness to move yourself into the future. To forgive is to start over, in a different place, to behave from the depths of your heart as if the bad thing never happened. In this sense, forgiveness is a creative act; for it asks that you create a new relationship. Starting now.

This requires a deep internal transformation. Forgiveness is not forgetting—papering over the words or actions that wounded you. Rather, it is being willing to expand your heart so much that you can look at the wounding thing from a different, elevated perspective. To lift yourself up from the good guy/bad guy view of life to the place from which you can realize that we are all trying as hard as we can, but we are all flawed. We all partake of the imperfections of the human condition, and we all have done or will do terrible, unforgivable things to one another.

Forgiveness asks that you see the person in the totality of his or her being, that you embrace your beloved in the whole range of his or her essence, understanding why he or she has done the wounding thing. Instead of remembering forever the petty crimes, insults, and abuses of the other person (and positing a future based on past disappointments and failures), forgiveness allow them to dissolve in the light of constantly renewing perception. In this sense, forgiveness invites you to start over, remembering again the good that was there all along, allowing the bad things to blow away like milkweed floss in the wind. ✪

ACKNOWLEDGE THE
POWER OF LANGUAGE
TO CREATE REALITY

*L*anguage is a very powerful instrument. What we utter is what we believe or expect, and if we say it enough, in time what we speak becomes true. What we say, and what we hear others say, has the power to sculpt our experience, our view of the world, and perhaps most important, our view of ourselves. One of the great gifts of love is that, in its midst, we can marshal this powerful capability and use it to bring life, enlightenment, and healing to the person we most adore.

One form of emotional healing comes from the precise use of language—words you speak and words that are spoken to you. Because of this, an intimate relationship and the verbal exchange intrinsic to it have a greater capacity than almost anything else in the world to heal us of deep emotional wounds.

Words spoken to us by our loved ones truly have the capacity to heal our memories and deeply imprinted pains and to recreate our sense of ourselves and of the world. This means that the negative words that shaped your early consciousness and/or your perception of yourself—"You're ugly"; "You can't have that; we're too poor"; "You never pay attention"; "Why can't you keep your mouth shut?"—can actually be revised, corrected, and dispelled through the careful use of language.

Scott had been endlessly yelled at for how he behaved at school, told what a mess he made of his schoolbooks, punished for being late, and criticized for getting Cs. Nobody had ever bothered to note his intuitive genius, the extraordinary function of his mind. Years of ravaged self-esteem began to be healed for Scott the day his sweetheart first told him he was intelligent.

"You're brilliant," she said. "I just love the way your mind works." "The minute she said that something inside me started to shift," he told me later. "I began to believe I wasn't stupid. The more she said it, the more I was able to believe her. And the more she said it, the more I noticed that other people sometimes said similar things. In time, her words changed how I felt about myself entirely."

Language does have the power to change reality. Therefore, treat your words as the mighty instruments they are—to heal, to bring into being, to remove, as if by magic, the terrible violations of childhood, to nurture, to cherish, to bless, to forgive—to create from the whole cloth of your soul, true love. ✑

SANCTIFY YOUR
RELATIONSHIP

*W*hether it is clearly visible or not, every relationship has a higher purpose than itself alone, a meaning that goes beyond the conventions of love and romance, and attaches the two people in it to a destiny that has roots in the past and wings in the future. This purpose is to shape us individually into the highest and best versions of ourselves and to change, if only in some tiny way, the essential character of the reality we have entered here by being born.

To know this is to believe that whatever occurs between you—the petty dramas and traumas, the life-shaping tragedies—is honing you for your unique participation in the human stream. It is to accept that the person you love has come into your life for a reason that goes beyond the satisfactions of the moment or even your personal future to reach into the web of time beyond time.

What you do here together, how well and how beautifully you do it, has implications not only for how cozily you sit together in your rocking chairs in your old age, but also for every other living being. We are all participants in the process of creating a species and a world that hums with peace and is informed by love. This is our highest heritage, and when we sanctify our relationships, the difficulties and insults they contain will be instantly diminished and what will stand in their place is the overwhelming presence of real love.

Sanctifying your relationship means seeing it not as an act of self-indulgence, but as an offering of love that you deliver up with joy to the fulfillment of its higher meaning.

This entails not only an attitude of acceptance but also two behaviors: making speech and keeping silence. It means verbally acknowledging this higher truth to one another: "Thank you for being the instrument for the discovery of my purpose." "I know we have come together for an important reason." "I love you for being my way to see the holiness of life."

At times it also means keeping the silence in your heart, which is a thanksgiving of this higher purpose, or engaging together in a practice meditation, which is a walking together in spirit, a prayer that your purpose together be revealed.

Your love is a stitch in the fabric of the All. To see it as such is to place your relationship in the ultimate perspective and to receive from it the ultimate joy. ☯

CONSECRATE YOUR RELATIONSHIP

*W*e all need the paths of our lives to be marked out so that we can be reminded of the quality of our lives and the beauty of our loves. We dignify and consecrate our relationships when we set them apart from the ordinary through ritual. Personal rituals provide a reference not only for the value we place upon our relationships, but also for the value we ask be conferred upon them.

When I was a child, my father would always say a prayer before dinner on my birthday: "With thanksgiving and love that you have been given to be a part of our hearts and of our family, we celebrate this day of your birth, beautiful child, delightful spirit. May you have a year full of joy and may your prodigious talents, like arrows, find their true mark through a long life in this world."

In the presence of these consecrating words, my life became more than simply the life I was leading. It became a holy place, with qualities and possibilities. It became a privilege and a responsibility. No matter what difficult times I came to, no matter what hardships I faced, the ritual of these consecrated words was a beautiful reference that pointed me to my higher purpose.

Relationships, also, should be consecrated in this way, made holy by the rituals and ceremonies that, in their mystical capacity, have the power to set them apart. Ceremonies say that, in effect, this day is not like all other days, this person is not like all other people; this love is not like all other loves. Not only in our hearts but also in our actions, we intend it to be a union of meaning, with allegiance to a lofty mission.

While we may think of consecration as something that can only happen in a church, we all have the capacity to hallow our relationships. The consecration of your relationship is a creative and deeply private affair. Set aside a special time to acknowledge your union—your wedding anniversary perhaps; designate a specific place in which to honor it; and create your own private ceremony—light candles, say words, play music.

Consecrating your relationship is the sign, repeated and beautiful, that you choose to view your relationship as holy, as no mistake, and that you intend, through it and with your beloved as your witness, always to live it to the highest of its purpose. 🕭

HOLD EACH OTHER
IN THE LIGHT

A relationship is always far more than we imagine or expect it to be. It is more than a living arrangement, more than being together in a social circumstance, more than the bright-colored kite tail of romance; it is the coming together of two persons whose spirits participate with one another, beautifully and painfully, in the inexorable process of their individual becoming.

In this respect, relationships are like relentless grinding stones, polishing and refining us to the highest level of our radiance. It is this radiance that is the highest expression of love—this is why a relationship is a spiritual enterprise.

When we look at the person we love with the expectation that he or she will or should solve all our emotional problems or make all our worldly dreams come true, we reduce that person to a pawn in our own self-serving plot, seeing the relationship as an experience of "What can I *get?*" rather than of "What can I *become?*"

When we view a relationship from a different vantage point—one that acknowledges it as a spiritual incubator—we come to see the person we love differently. We see him or her as separate from our hopes, from our demands that he or she be a particular way right now, for us. Rather, we recognize our sweetheart as a spiritual accomplice; we hold our beloved in the light.

Holding your love in the light is seeing the other as a soul in a constant state of becoming, encountering your beloved in all the radiance of his or her own being and strivings-to-be. To hold the other in the light is to seek the pure spirit that lies behind the limitations of individual psychology and social circumstance, to apprehend the full essence of your beloved, as she was since time began, as he shall be for all time after.

To do this is to reach beyond the petty and even gigantic disappointments that you experience in making your life together, to apprehend the divinity of this single unique and exquisite being who has been given to join you on the journey of your own becoming.

To hold each other in the light is to see one another as God would see you, perfectly engaged in the process of becoming perfect. ⓥ

SEEK YOUR
EMOTIONAL HEALING

*E*motional healing is the radical transforming of emotional wounds that results in the revivification of your body, the nourishment of your mind, and, ultimately, the illumination of your soul. In a sense, life itself is a healing journey through which we are moving from a state of forgetfulness about the true nature of our divine being and into a state of remembering and total illumination. It is because our emotions are the arena in which we can so often get derailed in this process that it is of such great importance that we seek our emotional healing. Since, in Western culture, we've been taught so much to perceive ourselves as emotional beings, we tend to stay focused on our emotional vicissitudes, and so long as we have unresolved conflicts on the emotional level, they will stand in the way of our moving on to the higher levels of love.

Sometimes we seem to be operating on the principle that everybody else was born perfect, and it's only a cruel quirk of fate that, unlike everyone else (all of whom are still perfect), we've got some ugly knots to untie. Not so. What is true is that within the basic perfection of the gift of life, we're all given certain difficulties, limitations, and problems as a kind of meditative theme to unravel throughout our lives.

Whatever we must heal—immobilizing fear,

explosive rages, abandonment in one or a hundred forms—is grist for transformation, opportunity for enlightenment. Each time we encounter one of these devastating limitations, we are invited to move through it and, once having healed it, to connect with a higher level of consciousness. On your journey, for example, you may be asked to expand your emotional repertoire from passivity to rage, from rage to forgiveness, from forgiveness to compassion, and from compassion to indivisible love.

Because love is our ultimate destination, this journey of healing is your life's true work. It doesn't matter whether you undertake it with additional help from psychotherapy, meditation, tai chi, weight lifting, Alcoholics Anonymous, the Baptist Church, vegetarianism, or an intimate relationship. Any path to healing, devotedly pursued, can deliver you to this destination—for there is no other. What does make a difference is whether or not you take the journey. If you don't, you will live awash in self-pity, endlessly tossed by your feelings, your unfinished emotional business. But if you do, you will see that what started out as your painful limitations became in the end your most radiant assets; and your soul, released at last from its endless emotional involvements, will emerge as the shining envoy of your love. ✿

BOW TO THE
MYSTERY OF LOVE

A relationship—two people coming together to live, to work, to play, to laugh, to grieve, to rejoice, to make love—is the form that human beings give to love, but love itself, that ineffable essence that draws us together into communion with one another, is beyond definition, beyond analysis. Love has its own way. Love just *is*.

Love is a mystery, the essence of which is angelic. In its very nature it goes beyond what we can understand by any of the systems through which we usually comprehend reality. It exists simultaneously outside us and within us. It both binds and frees us. It opens our hearts and breaks our hearts. It can neither be seen, except in the eyes of the beloved, nor felt, except in the heart of the one who is cherished. Invisible, its absence leaves us gray-hearted, wounded in spirit, while its presence transforms our hearts, our psyches, and our lives.

We seek love without knowing what it is, knowing we will know when we find it. This is the true mystery of love—that no matter how much we are unable to describe it, we always recognize it when we experience it.

Love infuses itself into relationships by means that are beyond our invention or imagining. Sometimes love comes to stay, nourished and coddled by the feelings and efforts of those who have invited it in. But if it is not honored or nurtured, love will go off to seek its true home.

In bowing to the mystery of love we acknowledge that love is beyond our comprehension, that we will never fully understand it. The love we seek seeks us, embraces us without our knowing, and binds our spirits into the body of itself. There is a point at which in the presence of love there is nothing more to say or prove, nothing left to ask for or regret, nothing left except the miracle of love itself. ✆

PART II

The Spiritual Journey of Love

It is our souls who choose us for each other.

We meet through the eyes and through the pulse.

We do not choose, but each is chosen for this love,

This path, this new green road, this kiss, this single beating heart,

This *us*.

Creating Depth

Depth is the soul's source,
the well from which
the heart draws up
great draughts of love.

APPRECIATE
THE MOMENT

This moment, this day, this relationship, and this life are all exquisite, unique, and unrepeatable. There will be no moment exactly like this one (the yellow light spilling in through the thin white louvers on the window, the sound of the men at work in the street and, in the living room, of the pages of the newspaper turning). There will be no day that repeats precisely the sweet events of this day (the waking and sleeping, the beautiful dreams before waking, the precious and even the ordinary conversations, the clothes you have chosen to wear, and the way that today you are wearing them, the way the wind is today, clattering the shutters, scattering the leaves, the thoughts—all 60,000 of them—that have passed like bright kites through your mind).

There will be no love, no dearly beloved, exactly like this one (the man who pronounces your name in just such a way, with his beautiful voice; the man who brings flowers, whose words move your heart so tremblingly softly, whose arms hold you this way and that way, embracing, consoling, protecting; the woman whose fragrance enchants you, whose head on your chest when you sleep is the sweet weight of bliss, whose kisses are blessings, whose laughter is sunlight, whose smile is pure grace).

There will be no lifetime exactly like this one, no

other, not ever again, not this birth, not this particular story, this mother and father, these houses and walls, these strangers and friends—and how we moved through it all, with such beauty, touching each other, dancingly stepping, curtsying, bowing across all the stages, filling the rooms of our lives with this joy, this sweet love. . . .

There will be no other way to live this life, only the way you have chosen to live it, only the way that, moment by moment, you fill up its houses and cradles and baskets, its cupboards and drawers—with which beautiful things, what small scraps and treasures—and only the way that you fill up your heart—with what feelings, which lovely emotions—and the memory of her standing there, in the light, by the window, her blonde hair in sunlight . . . and the image of him standing there and saying, "Always, forever, till death do us part"—and your mind—with what words, which endlessly coddled concerns, what difficult puzzles and brilliant solutions, what emptiness . . . waiting for God.

This moment, this day, this relationship, this life, are all unique, exquisite, unrepeatable. Live every moment as if you, indelibly, knew this. ☙

ASPIRE TO A SPIRITUAL
RELATIONSHIP

*T*o have a spiritual relationship is to consciously acknowledge that above all we are spiritual beings and that the process of our spiritual refinement is our one true undertaking in this life. When you have a spiritual relationship, you choose to embody this truth in love. You shift context and focus. Whereas an emotional relationship has as its focus the contents of the relationship itself, a spiritual relationship sees the spirit's well-being and the soul's journey as its overriding undertakings. Whereas the romantic relationship operates in time, the spiritual union has timeless infinity as its context. Rather than framing itself in life on Earth, it knows that we are all far more than we appear to be, and it joyfully claims as its territory a cosmos that radiates and scintillates, that includes an infinity of angels, and all the stunning coincidental events that are the mysterious instruments of God.

When you love one another in spirit, along with loving, desiring, cherishing, adoring, and protecting your beloved, you will also be the champion of your beloved's spiritual well-being, ensuring that she will make the choices that will allow for her soul's evolution. This may mean creating a quiet environment in which your spirits can flourish, or doing those things—meditating, praying, throwing away the television set—that will encourage a reunion of your souls.

To have an intimate relationship that is also spiritual defies our Western ordinary thinking, for, in a spiritual relationship, we are not seeking the satisfactions of the ego in a conventional way. Instead, we are aware that we are spirits and that we are on the spirit's journey.

The spiritual relationship is gracious, easy, considerate, and kind. Because it has stepped off the merry-go-round of ego concerns, it can be generous and patient, can behold the beloved not just as a person doing this or that, but as a soul on a journey. For, to the spiritually beloved, there is always a sense of this greater focus. Because of it, each action and experience takes on a different coloration. The disappointments of the moment and even the tragedies of a lifetime are seen not as happenings that are absolutes in themselves but finite, irritating specks on the larger screen of vision.

A great spiritual love does not exclude the psychological and physical—partners will always support each other in these realms with healing and attention—but when you love in the spirit, your love will also be a reminder of the infinite context, the true destination. Remembering this will give your love an exalted, crystalline, and truly luminous quality. For if your emotional relationship is a jewel, your spiritual relationship is the light that shines through it. ✆

REJOICE TOGETHER

*W*hen we think of being with one another emotionally, we ordinarily think of empathizing with one another in times of pain or misery. While it's certainly true that in our sufferings we have a great need for empathy, we also need positive empathy—rejoicing—a delighted feeling with and for all our joys.

Rejoicing is feeling joy, allowing the feelings of exhilaration and delight to enter your being and fill you with a fine, ecstatic sense of celebration. We all need to rejoice, to slather ourselves with exultation, because life is hard and at times our paths are very difficult. We need to rejoice because joy is our true state of being; and when we rejoice, we return to joy for a moment. We need to rejoice because there isn't enough rejoicing in the world. And we need to rejoice together because, in this world of self-involvement and nonstop competition, it's often hard to find a kindred soul with whom to rejoice.

Rejoicing is empathy at the encouraging end of the spectrum; and, although you may think it's easier to rejoice than to commiserate with someone, rejoicing, too, can be difficult. As a matter of fact, a lot of people feel so defeated in their own lives that instead of being able to celebrate with anyone else, they feel jealousy or self-pity. Indeed, unless you've really been able to feel your own joy, you may have a difficult time rejoicing, even with your beloved.

So, in order to rejoice together—to double your joy, to share your beloved's pleasures, and to truly celebrate them—allow yourself to rejoice first of all in your own life, about all the things that delight you, that brighten your day, that make your heart glad. Celebrate your victories; exult in your own achievements. Then you'll be well prepared to really rejoice with your sweetheart.

Rejoicing together is breathing in joy, being together at the moment of beauty (of soul-washing tears, of life-changing praise), in the hour of unbridled happiness, of sweet—or stunning—success. It is to be the loving witness at the epiphany of a talent (his book, her photography exhibit, his all-star game, her tennis match), to celebrate special occasions: birthdays, anniversaries, lifetime achievement awards. It is also to rejoice in all the cycles of your love—times and years you have shared, crises you have lived through, reunions that rekindled your love, and even all the good fights and their healing resolutions.

We must rejoice together because joy begets itself. It brings us more joy, more hilarity, a greater sense that life is radiance, splendor, pleasure, and fun. So one by one and, above all, together, rejoice! ☯

OPEN TO THE
ECSTATIC ENERGY

*L*ife is breath, movement. As long as you are capable of movement, you inhabit life and the energy of life inhabits you. In this state, every step you take, every word you utter, every thought that passes through the magic electronic circuitry of your brain, every single gesture you enact is an expression of your vivid aliveness, a sign that you are a mortal, alive human being.

In relationships, we join these energies with one another through passion and affection. Sexuality and sensuality are the media of our passionate connection, the arena where flesh and spirit meet; and affection is the medium through which we express our fond, caring love.

Sometimes in our overemphasis on verbal communication, we forget that we are also bodies and that as physical beings, too, we have a unique and powerful language. In our bodies, we "feel" and know things often before we can even begin to articulate them. Through our bodies, we share our love in an immediate, instinctual way that conveys a depth of feeling beyond words.

The language of the body is this energy, the invisible, ecstatic pulse that is the essence of life itself. We often think of our aliveness only as form—the bodies we inhabit—and not as the life force, or energy, that flows through them. In doing so, we miss feeling our own aliveness, and, in relationships, to be nourished by that mysterious spiritual commodity that is another person's "energy." Yet it is precisely the "energy"— of a city, a person, a piece of music, or an emotional exchange—that actually moves us at the deepest level. Nothing reveals this more clearly than a body which, through illness, is being drained of its energetic essence; and nothing demonstrates the presence of energy more dramatically than children.

In our intimate relationships, when we shift our attention from the material form—what we look like, what we're wearing, how in or out of shape we are— and move into the energetic realm, we enter the mystical arena in which we experience love itself as an expression of this energy. Instead of feeling it only as an emotion, we also sense it as an invisible pulse, the heart-filling throb, the luminous shivers that tell our bodies we have truly "felt" our love.

To move your focus from substance to energy and to seek the person whose energy, for you, is ecstatic, is to immediately expand your repertoire of love. When you do, you will not only be able to talk about the love you feel, you will actually be able to "feel" it as the tingling, brilliant, ecstatic presence in your body. So open your heart—and every cell of your being—to the luminous life-changing wisdom that is your soul's ecstatic energy. ✆

DISCOVER SEX
AS SACRED REUNION

*O*ur sexuality is one of the loveliest, most complex, and satisfying aspects of our intimate relationships. It is where we gather in the flesh to be joined, connected, and bonded. It can bring us joy or disappointment. It can be the source of our most painful betrayals, or of the highest moments of our ecstatic love.

Just as bringing our bodies together in the sexual encounter reminds us that we are bodies, essentially physical beings, so orgasm, the moment of blossoming ecstasy, connects us to the spiritual essence within us. Taken in total, making love is the movement of the mystic, electric current that bears eloquent witness to the fact that we are not just physical beings but temples wherein the spirit resides.

To apprehend your lovemaking in this way is to move toward the sacred in your sexual relationship. It is to ask more of it, give more to it, and receive more, far more, from it than you can ever expect from the how-to-improve-your-sex-life articles in popular magazines. Although handy-dandy advice columns and erotic manuals may indeed solve some of your sexual machinery problems, they will drop you off at the doorway of sex as a gymnasium, romance novel, or power trip, leaving you with only a sensate thrill. Thus you are denied the magnificent opportunity of experiencing your sexual encounters as a spiritual reunion of the highest order.

In making love, it is not only our bodies that are happily and deliciously engaged; but, because of the irresistible magnetism that sexual attraction is, we are also invited to contemplate in the mind and actually experience in the body the spirit which lives and moves within us.

Through sex we enter the timeless, boundary-less moment. We partake of the one experience above all others in life that allows us the bliss of true union. Here ego and all its concerns are erased, and the self is dissolved in utter surrender. To know, feel, and discover this in the presence of another human being, as we are invited to do in making love, is to be brought face to face with one of the greatest mysteries of human existence—that we are spirit, embodied, and that, as human beings, we are partaking in this miracle.

To experience your sexual relationship in this way is to elevate it to the sacred encounter it is. In so doing, you will experience your body as a vessel of the divine, your orgasm as a gift of the spirit, and your beloved as he or she with whom you are gifted to share a taste of eternal bliss. ☙

ACCEPT THE GLORIOUS
COMPROMISES OF LOVE

*T*here is a component of sacrifice to every intimate relationship, no matter how blissful or harmonious it may be. When you choose to love one person in a special, committed way, you are unchoosing—or giving up—your option to choose all others, for a time at least, in that same particular way.

Love—the feeling—and "being in love"—the ravishing experience—make us willing, even daredevilishly eager, to make these sacrifices. It's a joy to choose one above all others, a delight to feel graced and blessed by your beloved's uniquely delicious and heartwarming presence.

But this choosing, grand as it is and willing as we are to make it, is also symbolic of the many choices, little renunciations, and revisions of priority that, for love, we shall come to make as we walk the path of relationship. There's a great deal we do (or discontinue doing) precisely and only because we love. Joan postponed graduate school to care for Phillip's two children, whose mother had died of cancer. Mark moved out of the house he'd built for himself to live in the town where René, his new love, was a tenured professor.

Such revisions are only the tip of the iceberg. Each day, in love, you will be faced with decisions and choices, invited to make compromises that represent a willingness to meet your beloved halfway on the playing field of love. Thus, you may find yourself adapting to uncomfortable schedules or meticulous (or sloppy) housekeeping habits (the proverbial toothpaste folded up wrong—or far too perfectly), taking vacations you never imagined (but ended up loving anyway), preparing foods you never even liked, or entering into financial arrangements that stretch your equanimity to the limit.

A compromise—what you do for love—needs to be just that: a conscious revision of your own preferences. As such, it becomes a creative, imaginative act, an opportunity to expand, to experience life in a new and surprisingly beautiful frame. But above all, it shows you the depth of your love. For when we smooth off the corners of our own dogmatic priorities, we reach toward one another. In so doing, we see that love, the deep recognition of the soul of our beloved—and not all the compromises we have made—is truly what we have received. ✆

LIE IN THE ROSE PETALS

*W*ouldn't it be wonderful if you could just say, "Come lie with me in the rose petals"—if you had the rose petals to lie in, if you had enough time to lie down, sweetly, deliciously, in them, if you had the beautiful imagination to whisper such words in the first place.

To be able to say such words would mean that some wonderful things had already happened to you—that your spirit was already free, that your heart was open and clear, that you had already been touched so deeply, so dearly, by someone that you could want to lie down in a bed of rose petals with him, with her (feeling the texture, breathing the fragrance, savoring the mystic effervescence), that you have arranged your life, your day, your way of being so that, in fact, you could partake of your own wise and wild invitation.

To say, "Come lie with me in the rose petals" would mean that you have the courage to ask, to risk, to be foolish, to hope and expect, to want, and to wildly imagine, to magically dream.

Come, lie with me in the rose petals and let us bow down to the scent of the roses, perfuming our sorrows, diminishing the grasp of all our tragedies, unraveling the grip of all the ordinary awful tasks that bind us, dull us, and so tediously unshine us. Let us slip for a moment into the sweet bliss of roses, into a breathless bevy of kisses, of magic, of always. . . .

How long has it been since you've spoken such courtly, majestic, and fanciful words?

There is no time like this moment. There are no words more special than the ones you feel moved to utter, no risk more worthy than the one you fancy taking, to move you farther, more deeply, into the sweet bliss of love.

Therefore, take courage, be a jester and a hero, and say to your darling beloved (while the sun watches, while the moon hovers, while the birds sing), "Come lie with me in the rose petals, and let us rejoice in our love." ☙

SHARE YOUR
TRANSCENDENT MOMENTS

*A*t one time or another most of us will have what is sometimes called a "spiritual experience." One day, without trying or imagining, we will slip through the sieve of life as we ordinarily know it and into the experience of some mysterious happening. It may be a beautiful light, a feeling of infinite bliss, a coincidence so profoundly stunning as to convince us, absolutely, if only for a moment, that we are part of a world and a system of being so immense, so elegant, and so rarified in its extraordinary design that we bow before it, are awed and forever changed.

In the past we conceived of such things as happening only to mystics and saints, people whose whole lives were clearly set out on the spiritual path. But the truth is that what we refer to as a "spiritual experience"—a direct encounter with the mystery we inhabit and of which we are each a flawless part—is an event for which our whole lives are a metaphor and toward which our whole lives are leading.

Just as emotions are a natural expression of the personality, experience of the numinous—the sacred and exalted in our midst—is the organic experience of the soul. In fact, if you carefully ask each person you know, you will be surprised to discover how many people have already had an encounter with the sacred.

When you are gifted with such an experience, a

moment of touching transcendence, and when you share it with your beloved, you have, as it were, invited him or her to partake of the secrets of your soul. "As I lay on my bed, I felt a benign and beautiful presence enter the room. I thought perhaps it was death, but it was gentle, luminous, and kind. It stood beside me for a small, short while, granting me an unspeakable sweet experience of bliss, and then it was gone."

"I lay on the grass, staring mindlessly up at the clouds, when suddenly they parted and opened, revealing into my vision an ineffable, endless, radiant presence of light. I was bathed in the light; it subsumed me and carried me up, so that I wasn't myself anymore, but one with it."

Such breathtaking, sacred experiences are benedictions of the divine. Although we hear of them as isolated, extraordinary, or even "paranormal" events, none of us stands outside of their reach; for they are the true inheritance of our souls, and the more we are softly open to them, the more they will occur.

So share with your beloved your experience of the sacred. By so doing you will be reminded that the divine is always with us. We live in the midst of it; and it lives in the midst of us. ☯

BE AVAILABLE TO
THE MYSTERY

*L*ove of the heart and soul is mysterious. It takes chances. It believes in miracles. It is breath, movement, magic, music, the evanescent moment, the blissful surprise. To be available to the mystery means that you are open, expectant, waiting—continually poised on tiptoe, prepared to be illumined—not locked in your own expectations of how you think it should happen.

In life and in love, this means living free, with your mind set loose from its gears, not endlessly chattering inside, "But it has to be this way," or "I thought it was going to be that way." Our own ideas, those tidy little constructions of the intellect and psyche, just serve to limit our reality, shut down the possibilities, create a universe only as complex and rarified as the busy minds that invent it. Indeed, if we're too invested in the concepts of the mind, we will only recognize the things and allow into our lives the kinds of experiences that confirm what our minds have already seen.

When we set out to prove our presumptions, we scotch our chances of falling toward the miraculous. That's because being available to the mystery means being willing to believe that something more or different—something we literally cannot imagine—could be lying in wait for us. Indeed, when you surrender, you may step into an experience so huge and splendid and grand that, truly, you may feel as if you have stepped right out of this world. Yet miracles await us at every corner, in every dimension of our lives. We fall in love; our children are born; we stand on a street in a foreign city and meet the friend of a lifetime. Falling asleep, we dream, and in dreaming are given solutions to some of our knottiest problems. Whether in the unexpected and beautiful elevation of our daily lives as we ordinarily live them, or through the destined and magical introduction to a deeper life of the spirit, we are all being invited to come to the larger world, the brighter light, the truer home.

Indeed, as we move through life we are continually presented with events and encounters that, in defying our expectations, quietly nudge us to change. The degree to which they can change us depends on whether because of our minds we dismiss them, or whether, because of remaining beautifully open, we can receive what they are offering.

To be available to the mystery, therefore, is to be willing to be surprised—as a child discovers his face in the mirror; as a lover, undressing his dearly beloved, discovers the secrets of his adored. To be open to the miraculous is at last to be bountifully blessed. It is to move with grace, as you sweetly conduct your life, from the mountains of the mind to the rivers of the heart. ☙

KNOW ONE ANOTHER
LIKE THE SEASONS

*T*he journey of love is a journey of many sweet knowings. It is the sweet bliss, in first love, of discovering all your love's little secrets, her favorite flower and fragrance, the color that sets off her eyes so; his plaid flannel shirt, the way he laces up his boots, his shaving brush, and that one wild hair in his eyebrow; the scent of her skin, the feel of her hair, the drawer she keeps her lingerie in.

It is, later, the being together of love—the sound of the key as he locks up the house, of the rain in the shower each morning, as, singing, she washes her hair. It is how she rolls over at night in bed, how he sleeps, like a saint, with his hands folded over his chest; it is what he can fix; what she can mend.

And it is the changing, this way and that way. Arguing. There are the bad words, the anger and love in the midst; making love, holding hands. And the children, wanting, not being sure about wanting them; being scared, and so overjoyed, and seeing them sleeping and carried, at night, in his arms; how he is so tender, how she is so easy, so strong with them.

It is watching the years go. Come and go. Come and come. Go and go. Autumn and spring and winter and summer. So slowly and endlessly beautifully folding, unfolding. And so quickly go. And how we have done every year, so many things. And so few. Each day, and the meals and the work and the talk. Each day a small town with a map, and the trip we have taken in it. And the walks and the light, and the changing of the light. And how we have traveled. And how we have given the gifts. At Christmas. On birthdays. And all the words. The cards. The things we have said. The things we have whispered. I love you. Good night. I adore you. You are the one.

And how time has passed. He has grown old. And the white in his hair, and the fine, thin lines of his life and the sun are remaking his eyes; and her eyes, softer now, but still blue, and the so many years and the fading, and how the flower she loved and the color, and, yes, her perfume are still all the same; and how he still sleeps like a saint with his hands folded over his chest, and how the remembering now and forgetting are all a single long song, and how we have melted, woven ourselves, befriended, ensouled one another; how here at the end we know one another so well, like the bird knows the air, like the snowdrift knows the snow; and how he had said long ago, until we know each other like the seasons; and now it is spring now it is summer now it is autumn now it is winter; and we know we know we know. ✦

Finding Meaning

Love gives meaning
to our relationships.
Our relationships
give meaning to our love.

LIVE THE TRUTH

*T*here is nothing purer than the truth. It stands inviolate on its own merit, searing through falsehood and equivocation, shining brilliant as the spiritual totem around which our whole lives are organized. The truth is indivisible, stunning, eternal, the alpha and the omega of our mortal human existence. Nothing less than the truth can ever equal it; and nothing less than the truth can ever pass for it.

Living the truth is an occupation of the soul at every level and in every compartment of our being. To live the truth with oneself is itself a journey, a life's work of self-reflection and discovery. To live the truth with another is a journey of risk and compassion. It requires listening, being open. It includes the empathetic moment in which we surrender, expressing our own urgent truths in order to be present with another during the unfolding of his, or hers. To live in the truth with many others, with the larger whole of strangers and friends, or of the world community, is an exercise of the spirit. It asks us to grow, to expand. At times it may ask that we set aside or even see as inaccurate or wrong what we once perceived as the truth in our limited individual contexts.

Truth is a journey toward itself. To live in truth is to be aware that, as your context changes, so will your view of the truth and the range of the truth that your heart and soul can contain. Your truth may not be now what it once was or what it will be in the future; but it is your duty to live and speak your truth of the moment and to be willing to change it, should some larger truth be revealed.

In relationships, we begin with the small truths— what's true at the moment for us—and speak them, in love, to the persons we love. We start with our stories, our needs, our hopes, and our dreams, then move on, through the many and varied vicissitudes of our ever-unfolding personal selves, toward the truth that embraces us all. For the ultimate truth is immense; it swallows up all other truths, our little individual truths, the contradictions we all are living, and even the bigger truths of paradox and dogma, of principles and rules.

Begin your journey toward truth. Search for the truth inside you that is longing to be expressed and find the words to speak it. See the truth that stands in your midst, that is carried, embodied, and spoken by all your strangers and friends. Live the higher truth as you know it, as it is revealed to you—through art, in music, in literature, in nature, and in dreams. Receive the truth that surrounds you, for the truth is every-where. Surrender yourself to the truth, for truth is the ultimate light. Align yourself with the truth, for to live your life in the truth is to live in perfect freedom. ☺

SEE YOUR BELOVED
AS A SPIRITUAL BEING

We all know that there's more to a person than meets the eye, that we fall in love with the depth of a person, not just his or her surface attributes, and that there's something inside each person that calls us irresistibly, quietly to it. This is the spirit inside, the whisper of the divine that each of us contains.

It is connection with this essence that we seek in love, and falling in love is the moment when we are able to feel this divine whisper and see our beloved's spirit most clearly. In that sublime moment, we see in some way that's not quite magical—yet not quite ordinary either—that this particular human being is rare, beautiful, and fine in a way that goes far beyond all the specific things that we might say about him or her. In this moment we have in a sense relaxed our ordinary perception and seen "through the eyes of love."

The eyes of love are, in fact, the openhearted perceptions through which we are able to see not just the traits of personality but also the shining of the soul. With such vision we apprehend not just the surface things—what he's wearing, how much money she has—but, for a moment, our beloved's divinity.

To continue to see your beloved as a divine being means that, long after the rush and glow of that first perception have been dulled by the interference of the multitude of obligations and undertakings of your mutual life, you will still be able to turn, through the inner eyes of your soul, to the deeper truth of his being. You will see your beloved as radiant; as an infinite, beautiful soul; you will see her as the love she embodies; as the infinite joy that has found its home in him.

Unfortunately, as time goes on, we forget to practice this vision. Ordinary life takes over and we give ourselves over to it. Through the algebra of necessity, we replace the X of the divine in our perceptions with the ABCs of emotions and the demands of everyday life.

But you can train yourself to remember. If you hold your heart open just a little bit wider, then love will become your lens. A million problems will instantly vanish, and the scratchy difficulties of life as you normally live it will suddenly dissolve. By shifting your focus, you can look squarely, purely, into the eyes of the soul of this divine human being again.

There will be no differences then, between you and her, between you and him. Your differences will melt in the radiant sameness you are. And you will be left, in the light of your soul, with your mirror of the divine. ☙

HAVE THE COURAGE
TO SAY "NO"

*W*e are defined in life and in love not only by what we have the fortitude to undertake but also by what we have the courage to resist. In the long-ago movie, *Days of Wine and Roses,* a man and woman descend into a wildly gyrating spiral of alcoholism, all the while egging each other on. Finally, the man says "No" to himself, then, eventually, to his wife.

Life doesn't always ask us for such intense denunciations, nor is the path to our *No*'s always so excruciatingly painful. But we all have things that we have to say "No" to—for ourselves and in our relationships—or else move in a direction that isn't for our highest good.

Sometimes these *No*'s are small and simple, an unadorned statement of preference that's a quiet affirmation of your right to be yourself: "No, I don't want to go to the late show; I'll be too tired for work in the morning." "No, I don't want dessert." "No, I don't want to go to the party." Sometimes they ask for more strength, require that you actually take a stand: "No, I don't want to buy a.... We're already too much in debt," or sometimes, as in the unforgettable movie, they involve issues of life and death: "No, I won't give up my AA meeting just because you'd like me at home on Tuesday night."

Having the courage to say "No" means that you

trust yourself and your relationship. It means you believe that your bond has the strength and resilience to absorb your "No," as well as the power, as a consequence, to grow—in well-being, in moral fortitude. In saying "No," you exercise the faith that the two of you, together, can live by the values represented by your *No*; recognizing that these values will take you to a level higher than the one embodied by the things that you are choosing to resist.

Sure, we could have five more drinks and lose consciousness. Yes, we could tell a lie and lose our integrity. Yes, I could capitulate to all your preferences and then resent you because I did.

A *No* is a choice for the good, the true, and the beautiful thing, and, in relationship, for the power, the beauty, and the possibilities of the relationship itself. Have the courage to say *"No!"* ✪

ACCEPT WHAT IS

We usually mosey into relationships seeing their obvious possibilities, imagining specified outcomes, cocooning them with our own expectations. But what actually occurs is often shockingly different from what we expected. The person you wanted to marry has a phobia about commitment. The woman you knew would make a great mother decides to go off to law school. The suitor with the bottomless trust fund decides to give away all his money and live in a cave. Surprising revisions can happen on even the simplest levels: "When I fell in love with him, he was wearing a blue cashmere blazer and gray flannel slacks; but after I married him, all he would wear was sweatshirts and blue jeans."

Expectations come in two forms: general and specific. General expectations have to do with our dreams and plans for a specific relationship—that it will lead to marriage, that it will bring you children, that it will make you "happy." Specific expectations have to do with what we think we can count on day to day—he'll take out the trash, she'll handle the kids in a way I approve of. On one level, these expectations are all quite reasonable; it's appropriate to have long-range plans and goals, and it's legitimate to expect specific kinds of participation from your partner.

But when your relationship becomes a litany of failed expectations—what you hoped for but didn't get—it's time to look at what's happening from an entirely different perspective. Perhaps, instead of needing to "communicate better" or "negotiate your differences" on an emotional level, you're being asked, on a spiritual level, to learn to accept what is.

Accepting—finding a way to be comfortable with things as they are—is actually a very developed spiritual state. It means that you've relinquished the pre-conceptions of your ego and surrendered to what's been given to you. Maybe he's not the provider you hoped for, but his spiritual strength is a constant inspiration; perhaps she's not the housekeeper you wanted, but the way she nurtures your children is absolutely beautiful.

Acceptance allows your spirit to grow. When you're able to recognize the little miracles and great lessons that replaced your expectations, you suddenly discover that what you hoped for was pitifully puny compared to what was actually held in store for you and that, in a way far more complex and elegant than you yourself could have imagined, your life is following a sacred design.

So if you want a life that is larger than life and a relationship that is finer than even your wildest hopes, peel back your expectations and start to accept what is. ☺

RESPECT
THE OPPOSITE SEX

*I*t is certainly sad and seems almost strange that we must actually encourage or instruct ourselves to respect the opposite sex. Yet, unfortunately, because for decades we have been so bombarded with attitudes, articles, and books that underline the differences between men and women, we now live in a world where we are surrounded by antagonism between the sexes. For the sake of union—in society and in our intimate relationships— we really must consciously choose now to honor the opposite sex.

Honoring means remembering the value of, cherishing, holding dear, celebrating rather than disparaging the differences between, remembering the beauty, enjoying all the contrasts, savoring in clarity the blessings of the other. It means not building walls out of differences, but delighting in each beautiful, amusing one as the counterpart and balance to our own splendid gender's hilarious uniqueness.

It also means moving from the surface to the depths, realizing that beneath the familiar costumes of gender we all embody a similar evolving consciousness, that inside we all carry as great emotional treasure the same exquisite array of feelings. A man's grief over the death of his father is no less real than a woman's grief over the loss of her mother. A man's heart will be as poignantly, beautifully touched by a breathtaking sunset, the rustle of cottonwood leaves in Yosemite, or a cool, crystalline autumn morning as a woman's. At the core we are all moved by our sorrows and by the magnificence and miracles that touch us, not as men or women, but as human beings.

To know this is to relax the wearying focus on our differences, to come graciously into the knowing that we can honor one another without harming or short-changing ourselves. It is to remember that what we live and suffer, we live and suffer in common, and that real love, love in the soul, is beyond male and female, beyond gender as an issue at all. ☺

TELL YOUR BELOVED
YOUR STORY

*E*specially if we've been connected for a long time, we think we know each other. We do, of course, know a whole array of things about one another, but it's really only when we tell our stories— the touching vignettes that embody our struggles, sweet moments, disappointments, or wild hopes and dreams—that our most real, most vulnerable selves are revealed. Indeed, if we don't tell each other our stories, we're all one-dimensional, blank screens on which we project our assumptions about one another.

Everybody has a story, and because we all do, when we hear each other's stories, we feel suddenly connected. Story is the great river that runs through the human landscape, and our individual stories are the little creeks that flow through us all to join the river at its source. When you tell your story, however, you open yourself to the level of fragility that, as human beings, we all share; for, no matter how different our stories, at the bottom of them all is the well of pain from which we have each dipped a draught.

Tell your darling your story—the most painful event of your childhood, the most exciting moment, the greatest regret of your adult life—and you will discover, in depth, a self you never knew. That's because between the sentences of our stories the gist of things slips out, not merely the facts, but the feelings that have shaped us, the point, in anyone's journey, from which there was no return.

For example, although you may be aware of your husband's fascination with architecture, you may not understand why he never pursued it, until you hear the story about the night his father got so angry at him for staying up late drawing that he broke all his drafting pencils, threw them the trash, and raved, "Since you're wasting your time like that, you're never going to get a cent to go to college." Or, you may know about your wife's interest in astronomy but not know where it came from, until you hear the story about how, when she was a little girl and heard her parents downstairs arguing at night, she would lie in her bed looking up at the stars until—she could swear—the stars beamed their white light right into her room so she could finally go to sleep.

When you tell your personal tale, spinning and spinning, telling, retelling, the tight thread with which you have wrapped up your pain will gradually start loosening. And when you listen to your beloved's story, he or she will become, in the process of your listening, a fully formed human being. So tell each other your stories. They're more than entertainment for the dinner table or a long ride in the car. They are your true selves, spelled out and spoken, brought forth in time and in your own language, a loving gift you give to each other. ✑

BE CONSCIOUS OF YOUR
UNCONSCIOUS

*C*onsciousness, being aware and being aware of your awareness, is a gift of the human condition. It is in consciousness, the state of being awake, that we act, we choose, we behave. We do what we are "conscious" of, draw from choices we actually recognize, behave in ways we realize we are behaving, and see that the outcomes we intended materialize into being.

But fluttering beneath consciousness lies the murky sub-basement of the unconscious. Here the memories, experiences, and events that have shaped our lives lie deep within us as the hidden motivations that are quietly directing our behavior all the time.

We all have a great many things stored in our unconscious—hurts of childhood so exquisitely cruel that we can't consciously remember them, a multitude of little stinging events that affected us deeply—but we really don't know quite how. Because we haven't dredged these things up for conscious examination, and healing, often, we can, with unconscious carelessness, hurt ourselves and others with them.

When a hurt or fear from childhood is randomly stimulated ("He rearranged the furniture three times, and I was scared that, just like my father, he'd never be satisfied with anything"), we may instantly attack ("I can't believe you spent all day redoing the living room. You're insane!") or do any number of other hateful things.

Unconscious behaviors have an uncanny power to direct—and undermine—our lives. Whether or not we know by name all the mad dogs roaming around our unconscious, it's our duty to be aware (on the conscious level) that there is a pack of mad dogs down there. We are responsible to ourselves—and to those we love—for our unconscious as well as our conscious behaviors. Unconsciousness is no excuse; in fact, in relationship, it is the supreme irresponsibility.

Little slights of the unconscious are the normal mistakes of not being able to empathize fully or of letting out small bits of anger in little unconscious acts—"I forgot"; "I didn't mean to"— but big deeds of the unconscious amount to interpersonal crimes, and we are responsible—and fully culpable—for them. In this realm exist the vast array of acts that run the gamut from the wife who flirts at a party because she's angry at her husband for being so late coming home to the father who beats his son to a pulp because earlier that day his boss lambasted him.

We all have things that can turn us into monsters, and some of our unconscious acts can ruin our relationships (to say nothing of our lives). Therefore it behooves you to discover your deep secret motivations, for in relationship (and in life) we are absolutely accountable for committing such personal "unconscious" crimes. ✺

SEEK THE COMMON
GROUND

*I*n the tit-for-tat world of our psychological dramas, we tend to make life adversarial. We take sides. We look at intentions and effects—she was late just so I'd feel bad; he said that just to hurt me. We seek redress for our insults and wounds; we keep score (you were late more often than I was; you bounced more checks than I did; you hurt me more than I hurt you; you're meaner than I am; well, anyway, you were meaner more times than I was).

It's as if in trying to find peace in our relationships, we think keeping score will win the day. If I treat you like an enemy, show you all your crimes, and prove that you're guilty, you'll decide to make up for it by loving me more because you feel so badly about how gruesomely rotten you've been.

Unfortunately (and fortunately), a lover or sweetheart isn't like a corporation that can be sued (and required to make recompense) for a faulty product. We don't "pay up" in love because we're shamed or proven guilty. In fact, the stronger inclination is to get away from the heat and head for the hills. Taking an adversarial position will only make an adversary of your mate; and adversaries make war, not love.

That's why, when conflict arises, we need to look for the common ground. In the midst of the fray, when we seek the kernel of truth that can bridge us to understanding, we can find our way back to union.

We all have a dark side; we've all hurt one another more than we'd like to admit. But even our misdeeds merit an attempt at understanding, because the truth is that even dastardly acts are born of pain. That doesn't excuse them, of course, but it's important to remember that even the difficult, hard, hurtful things we do to each other spring from the woundedness within us. When I can comprehend your suffering (and, therefore, the crooked behavior you perpetrated on me) and you can comprehend my pain (and, therefore, my wrongdoing to you), we can stand face to face in compassion, unravel the missteps we've made, and together start over from a different place.

So if, in your heart of hearts, you seek union, pleasure, companionship, support, and nourishment from your beloved, don't make an adversary out of him or her. Even in the hairiest fray, try curiosity and kindness—"Why were you late?" "Why were you so short with me?"—and you may find out something surprising ("I got back a frightening mammogram today"; "The guy right next to me in the gym keeled over and died"), something which, instead of turning your beloved into the enemy, will fill your heart with compassion. ✺

HOLD YOUR BELOVED IN
SPECIAL AWARENESS

*W*hen you love someone at a soul level, you carry a very special awareness on behalf of that person. In the deepest abyss of your being, you have agreed to know, see, sense, and feel for your beloved with a subtle kind of attention that continually takes the truth of his or her being into account.

The attention we carry for one another in this way runs the gamut from holding a quiet place in your heart so your beloved can go through his emotional healing to knowing that the person you love needs money, time, or space, even when she isn't consciously aware of it and can't ask you for it directly. Sometimes our refined perception takes the form of "just happening by" at the moment of crisis. At others, it may mean holding the awareness that the person you love has issues about her health, weight, body image, or a particular physical feature, and acting sensitive and supportive around that particular issue. You may hold your beloved's truth in awareness by recognizing that the person you love has a deep fear of abandonment to which you respond by being realistically reassuring, generous, and steadfast in your expressions of love, or by knowing that your sweetheart has been sexually abused and consciously encouraging him to discover his boundaries or seek her own emotional healing.

Sometimes we carry this awareness consciously; at

other times our awareness is secret even to us, a brilliant act of intuition that just seems to occur. The man who brings home flowers "for no reason" only to discover that minutes ago his wife received news of her mother's sudden death has unconsciously "sensed" her pain and met her need before she could even express it. Similarly, the woman who "doesn't know why" but shows up at her husband's office with lunch only to find out that earlier that morning his biggest deal of the year fell apart is also acting on an intuition unconscious even to herself.

This sort of intuitive second-guessing is a gift of love. It means that, rather than expecting your beloved to know, recognize, understand, and consciously verbalize every single thing that he or she needs, you will step in at times, recognizing the unspoken, and address it with your own intuitive kindness and care.

Is this codependence? Not if it's offered in consciousness (rather than out of dependence or low self-esteem); not if it's given in full awareness, as a conscious act of love; and not if you can accept it when it's given to you in return. ☺

MOVE TO THE
SPIRITUAL LEVEL

*W*e all come to terrible impasses in our relationships—fights we have over and over again, stubborn character flaws that just won't budge, irritating habits that can almost drive us crazy. When we sit in the midst of these things, we can feel angry, bitter, and stuck. In our minds we recite the ways we've been wronged, how terrible he or she's been, how hopeless our relationship is.

The truth is that we've all been wronged; and seemingly unbearable things do happen. There are issues in our relationships that we do go 'round and 'round on, and no matter how much we "work on," negotiate, talk about, or attempt to solve them, we don't seem to make much progress.

At such times, we can feel really discouraged or we can look at our relationships through a different lens. Instead of seeing them as existing to satisfy our every whim, we can lift them up to the spiritual level and ask ourselves what it is that we're being invited to learn. If you thought of the problem as a lesson, what would it have to teach you? If you thought of it as a divinely ordained detour, what might it be saving you from? If you construed it to be an invitation to grow in some new direction, what would that be? By lifting it up to the spiritual level, you can begin to see everything that occurs in your relationship as an opportunity for spiritual growth.

That's because whatever is happening in a relationship is happening simultaneously on emotional and spiritual levels. When you view it only on the psychological level, you can keep going around and around in a rat's nest of unresolved problems. But when you lift it up to the spiritual level, let it ascend to where the bright light of truth can shine in, you will, I assure you, see something quite different. There, instead of focusing on the nuisance of the moment as this week's edition of the hopeless situation, you will see that every event in your relationship is something that showed up to expand, inform, or refine you. Instead of endlessly blaming yourself—or your beloved—for the difficulties that inevitably transpire, you will see them as serving a higher purpose—the development of your soul.

When we move to the spiritual level, we recognize lessons, instead of blaming for errors and mistakes. We see our partners no longer as those who fail to fulfill all our hopes and dreams, but rather as those whose spiritual task it has been to embody the very frustrations through which (by struggling and chafing against them) we develop spiritual maturity. This also eases us on the emotional level, for when we can feel compassion instead of judgment—for ourselves and our beloved—our relationships become instantly sweeter, deeper, and more gracious. ♥

PROTECT YOUR SOUL

The journey of the soul is not all joy, nor is it always consummated in the light, for in this life we make a choice at every moment of what our soul's destination shall be. Just as in a dance one may move in any direction—forward and sideways, fly beautifully elevated or be bowed down toward the Earth—so in life do we also, constantly, through every infinitesimal increment of our behavior choose a direction, the path our souls will take.

If a man kills his wife and uses the legal system's loopholes to escape conviction, he has not only gotten away with murder, he has lost his soul. He may be set free, return to the usual circumstances of his life, but he will never be free; he will be a soulless man whose very existence is the embodiment of untruth. No matter how many people he may falsely convince of his innocence, in the light of the truth he is still condemned; and should he try insanely to convince himself of his own innocence, then surely his soul shall be lifted by the darkness from him.

There is no neutral moment or action in our experience. Everything we do, every action we enact, every nuance of movement, each word we utter either creates the further illumination of our souls or moves us in a direction in which, in a moment of dark unconsciousness, our souls can be utterly compromised.

The potential for loss of soul—to one degree or another—is the affliction of a society that as a collective has lost its sense of the holy, of a culture that values everything else above the spiritual. We live in such a spiritually impoverished culture—and in such a time. Loss of soul, to one degree or another, is a constant teasing possibility. We are invited at every corner to hedge on the truth, indulge ourselves, act as if our words and actions have no ultimate consequence, make an absolute of the material world, and treat the spiritual world as if it were some kind of frothy, angelic fantasy. In such a world the soul struggles for survival; in such a world a man can lose his own soul and have the whole culture support him, and in such a world, conversely, the light of a single great soul that lives in integrity can truly illumine the world. ✿

Enhancing Intimacy

Intimacy is connection,
the weaving together of our
two souls into a single beautiful
cloth. It is the pattern of that
cloth, the music we play
as we spread the cloth
on the table and set
it with goblets and
wait for the feast
to begin.

PURSUE BEAUTY

*B*eauty is luminous radiance. Beauty is lucent, mystical essence, the face that is unforgettably lovely, the dance with the exquisite movements that our minds cannot erase, the music whose notes repeat themselves endlessly in our hearts. Beauty infuses; beauty enthralls; beauty inspires and illumines; beauty lifts up and enlivens our souls.

Beauty applies to both the material and the ethereal worlds. Beauty calls on our organs of perception (She's a beautiful woman) as well as our spiritual sensitivity (It was a beautiful experience) and mystically coordinates these worlds for us. Whereas beauty is embodied in form, the apprehension of beauty, whatever its form, is an experience of transcendence. It is this remarkable capacity of beauty to be at once both immanent and transcendent that causes us to pursue it, to be moved by it, and to recognize that in some ineffable way we can trust it as the measure of what has value for our souls.

Beauty also enchants us because its essence is to embody more, a higher level of whatever it is that we are perceiving. In standing above all others, the beautiful thing invites everything around it to rise to its own level. So it is that the beautiful moment teases us to make all moments beautiful, the beauty of the written word to elevate our own language, the sound of beautiful music to surrender to the beautiful soundless stillness in our own hearts.

When we have soul-filling experiences in nature, when we lose ourselves in the ecstasy of orgasm, at times of searing joy, when the veil is lifted and we glimpse the sacred frame of life, we are experiencing beauty, a taste of our true eternal state of being.

We often step into a relationship for some quality of beauty it contains—she was beautiful; he was playing beautiful music when you first walked into his rooms; he has a beautiful heart; she has beautiful hands—and it is this same quality, beauty, that will elevate your relationship and cause it to ascend. Great beauty is both a gift to be received and a state to be pursued.

So fill your life with beauty. Allow your beauty to shimmer forth. Anoint your house with beautiful things: objects, fragrances, movements, moments, sounds, emotions. Beautiful food is a sanctification of the body. Beautiful ideas are a feast for the mind. Beautiful art and music are a banquet for soul. We must seek beauty, respond to it, cultivate it, and surround ourselves with it, for beauty in this life is a reflection of our souls, as our souls shall be forever a pure reflection of it. ☙

BE PATIENT, GENTLE,
AND KIND

*P*atience is a quiet virtue, the ability to willingly wait for what is unseen to gradually be made manifest. Patience is faith, the conviction that what you imagine, need, or believe to be the highest fulfillment of how you think things ought to be—for yourself, for your relationship, for the whole amazing span of your life—will gradually and beautifully reveal itself in time. Patience with one another is also a quietness of spirit, a deep inner knowing that rests secure in the knowledge that you are on the right journey, that your beloved is with you, and that no matter the pitfalls or detours, you can stand at his side, be in her presence, quietly waiting ... with patience.

Gentleness is the soft virtue, the cloudy featheriness of spirit that allows you to move toward the person you love, and through each circumstance you face, in an easy, graceful, and gracious manner—touching delicately, listening openly, feeling with empathy, seeing with eyes of compassion. Gentleness eases the way, adds refinement and grace to the journey, softens the blows, cushions the sorrows, lightens the burdens.

Gentleness can be everywhere: in what we say, in how we move, in the people and circumstances we quietly choose to bless ourselves with. It is moving easily instead of roughshod through life; speaking with kindness rather than blurting things out; leaving time instead of blusteringly rushing through things; making room for the stranger who arrives, the beautiful thing that unexpectedly happens.

Kindness is the sweet virtue. It soothes and calms and renews. It remembers, adds touches of color—blankets and bed socks and flowers. It offers the unasked-for word, the spirit-cleansing compliment, the nurturing embrace. It is soft; it reaches out to mend and amend: Can I help you? Is there anything I can do? I'm sorry. I hope things will change. Kindness is the unnecessary necessity, the unasked-for moment of beauty that adds a hopeful texture to every measure of our lives.

Love waxes and wanes with the seasons, with our hormones, and our circumstances, but love of the heart and soul must be constantly nourished and tended. Patience gives us hope for the future; gentleness gives us grace in the moment; kindness dissolves the wounds of the past. Be patient and gentle and kind, and the love you hold as a treasure now will beautifully flourish and last. ☞

TAKE CARE OF
YOUR BODY

*W*e often think of our bodies as our own private possessions, and, of course, in a fundamental way, they are. But when you're in a relationship, your body is also the medium of your connection to your beloved. If you didn't have a body, you wouldn't be here to love anyone in the first place; and it is your body, your physical presence, with which the person you love is continually engaging. After all, it's your body you bring home from work every day; it's your body that sleeps with your darling at night. You have to look in the mirror to actually see how you look; but the person who loves you has to look at you all the time. When you're exhausted or depressed, your darling will see the weariness in your face, your stance, just as he or she will also recognize your sense of well-being, vitality, and happiness.

Because of this, the way you treat your body carries great significance in any relationship. It can be a gift, an asset, a joy, a grand celebration for your beloved, or a detriment, a burden, the occasion for a spiritual test. Just as radiant health and well-being can present beauty and inspiration to the person you love, so physical self-abuse or neglect can become the reason that your relationship starts to break down. If you don't take care of your body, you're sending a message both to yourself and your beloved—because how you take care of your body is a reflection not only of how you feel about yourself but also of how you expect your sweetheart to feel about you. If you're in the process of destroying your body in one way or another (by smoking, drinking to excess, being a workaholic or a sugar, caffeine, or sit-down-at-the-desk-and-never-get-any-exercise addict), how can you reasonably expect your darling to delight in and enjoy your body or to reflect to you the love you haven't been able to give to yourself?

In sharing your body with the person you love, you are sharing your true essence. So honor that essence, the highest human expression of your embodied soul, by nourishing, loving, and cherishing your body—for yourself and for your beloved. ☺

PRACTICE THE ART
OF EMPATHY

*F*eeling with and for someone—having empathy—is the deepest form of emotional participation that you can have with the person you love. In your intimate relationship it can make you feel more known and knowing, more fully recognized and seen, more beautifully, deeply connected.

Empathy is emotional engagement. It is entering the badlands of another person's emotions and camping out there with him, allowing yourself to feel what he feels, to be moved as she has been moved, to fear, grieve, and rage as if you yourself had been touched, frightened, bereaved, or driven to anger.

Having empathy isn't necessarily easy. Indeed, of all the emotional interventions, empathy is the most demanding. For to actually be able to enter into another person's experience so fully that she is able to feel your presence there with her is the embodiment of the highest degree of emotional refinement. To truly join your beloved—in the place of his powerlessness, or of her shame—is to have already, in some sense, visited these hellish realms on your own.

The supporting cradle of empathy is constructed from the huge array of feelings we have already felt in our own hearts and bodies. If you haven't first felt a particular feeling, or if you're unwilling to revisit it, your capacity to feel with another will be fuzzy, half-hearted, and dull. Your empathy will be a feeble attempt at sharing the feeling, not a truly empathic experience.

That's why empathy is such hard work. You have to do your own work first, to acquaint yourself, in depth, with your own emotions. Only then will you have, as it were, an *Encyclopedia Britannica* of the human feelings to refer to; because you have felt, you will "know what it feels like." You'll have a reference in your own body, an idea in your own mind, of how a particular experience is likely to feel to another person. Since you've "been there," you can truly empathize.

Unfortunately, one of our inhibitions in the practice of empathy is that we're often afraid of revisiting our own emotions when someone else is in need. Instead of being able to step into another person's experience, we're so afraid of being overwhelmed by the conscious recollection of our own painful feelings that instead of offering empathy, we deny ("It's not so bad"), problem solve ("Here's what to do"), or minimize ("You think that's bad? Let me tell you about what happened to me").

To be capable of empathy, therefore, become the master of your own emotions, not in the sense of control, but in the sense of allowing your feelings to flow through you. Then you'll be able to give that most precious of all emotional gifts—the gift of empathy. ☺

LIGHTEN UP!

*L*ife is miserable, boring, serious, and awful enough that you don't have to be so uptight, logical, organized, responsible, and on-time-all-the-time. Lighten up!

Yeah, but what about ... the dwindling dollar, the falling Dow Jones average, your dog's license, your driver's license, the registration for your car, income tax, the rent, dental problems, medical problems, lawsuits, marriage counseling, your aging parents and their problems, your teenaged children and their problems, the 2 million problems left over from your childhood that you still haven't solved, not to mention where the clean shirts are, where your car keys are, and what about that ugly stain on the rug....

You will never run out of things that have to be handled in this life. And they will never give you joy. There will always be a few more clothes to pick up at the cleaners; the checkbook will always need to be balanced. Before, during, or after doing any of these things, you will not feel particularly happy—they won't light up your life.

What will light up your life are the sweet things, the beautiful small things that bring stinging half-tears to the edges of your eyes. What lifts your heart in the moment? What are the beautiful things you remember from two hours ago? *Such a touching conversation with a stranger, her voice like the thin, broken*

feather of a bird. I could feel her courage. She cried a lit-
tle, talking about a song she wanted to write. It would be
about ordinary things, she said . . . like love.

What is memorable from yesterday? *The way the*
light was, orange edging the blue in the late afternoon,
and how in the light you could feel the coolness of the
air, how for a moment temperature and color were the
same.

What do you remember from the past five years?
How he loves me and what a surprise it is that he
does. . . . I had never imagined. . . .

They are not responsibilities, any of these things
that brushingly, beautifully, touch your soul, that
make you feel dancey, that sparkle your heart. They
are silly and priceless and foolish and free. Lighten
up! ☮

NOURISH YOUR HEART
AND SOUL

*W*hen we identify too strongly with the material world, we can lose track of our precious hearts and souls. We can almost begin to believe that it's the things of that world—objects and possessions—that will bring us happiness. The truth is that it isn't things but experiences—the moments and feelings that move us most deeply—which truly connect us to our real selves. Discovering what these things are is a process in itself, and partaking of them with your beloved is one of the deep joys of relationship.

To nourish your heart and soul, you must first comprehend that your heart and soul require great nourishment. Once you have understood this, you must make time and room for the things, experiences, and people who feed you deeply in these realms.

Nourishment of the heart is sweet personal love, the endless, sensitive play and interplay of all the emotions that exquisitely fill us and charm us, the sense that we are desired, that we have been chosen above all others to be loved, that we are one of a kind, irreplaceable, precious, and rare. Romance, sweet gifts, sensitive words and affectionate touches, beautiful evenings and sweet afternoons, elegant moments, a fabulous passion also awaken this love of the heart.

The food of the soul is more rare. Our souls are

nourished through mystery, through the experience of beauty, through witnessing and partaking of things and experiences that, in themselves, carry a reference to the eternal—great music, color, the fragrance of roses, mountains; the meadows, trees, and rivers that long ago held great meaning for us. Although these things have always been here to partake of, it is the way in which we experience them in elevated moments that allows them to speak to our souls of the unseen world, the unheard sound, the bliss we cannot yet feel but can only vaguely imagine. When we slip through the sieve of our ordinary lives and fall into the bottomless depths that these experiences open to us, we pierce, if only for a moment, the illusion that life as we know it is all there is.

For each of us there are such things. Some appear unasked for as gifts—others we must consciously pursue; but no matter how they come to us, when we are fed in this way, we sense instantly that we have been truly nourished. The famished heart can give no love; the starving soul can neither imagine nor remember its own sacredness. Indeed we cannot love truly until our own hearts and souls have been filled.

So put yourself in the presence of the things that nourish your heart, that can beautifully feed your soul. Drink deeply on your own and also with your beloved. Separately and together, nourish your hearts and souls. ☙

REDISCOVER
THE HARMONY

*H*armony is the spiritual beauty of any intimate relationship. It is elegant coexistence, peaceful compatibility, a similarity of frequency. It's knowing that you share the same view of the world, that what you want out of life runs along parallel lines. It's looking at your beloved and being able to say to yourself, "We stand for the same things, don't we? We may encounter some rough spots, but at heart we both share the same values."

In relationship, harmony is a gift of the spirit. It is a mystic similarity of essence that allows you to operate—both separately and together—from the comfortable wellspring of knowing that between you there is a sacred resonance. In a sense, it's the very reason you chose each other in the first place—if there weren't a certain degree of harmony between you, you wouldn't have thrown your lot in together and established a relationship.

When there's harmony, you can feel it; it will add grace to all your undertakings—your work, the rearing of your children, the way you conduct the actions of your daily life, the way you handle conflict, and what you perceive to be the underlying deep direction of your life.

Unfortunately, life scratches and claws at the harmony of our relationships. Too many demands in too many forms can undermine the pleasant ground of any union's harmoniousness. Schedules, children, unexpected little assaults from others can all make us feel at times as if there's no harmony left between us.

Conversely, harmony is nurtured and restored by being lovingly remembered. So if the harmony is out of balance in your relationship, ask yourselves the following questions: After all the fuss and fray, when the kids are in bed, when the fight is over, is the stream of our life together most of the time so good, so flowing, that, in general, I can give thanks for his or her presence in my life? In what ways are we, at the core, a complement, a mirror, a balance for one another? What things still give us pleasure together? What is the higher purpose of our relationship and what is our common undertaking?

If you have a hard time finding answers to these questions, take a good look at what's compromising the harmony in your relationship. Is it something you can change? Is it circumstantial—your wife's been on the road for a month—or is it an emotional issue that needs to be dealt with? What is the one thing you could do or say right now that would be a first step toward restoring harmony?

Harmony is the spiritual balance in any good relationship. So give thanks for the harmony you have, develop the harmony that's missing, and nurture the harmony that ensues. ✍

LET GO OF IT ALL

*W*hen in doubt, let go—give way; give in. When in expectation, frustration, or pain; when in confusion, impatience, or fear; when you don't know what to do next; when you're losing control—let go. Let go. Let Go. *Let Go.*

Letting go is emotional and spiritual surrender. It means willingly jumping out of the lifeboat of your preconceptions of reality and taking your chances out in the open sea of anything-can-happen. It means that even as your definition of reality is dissolving before your very eyes, you willingly relinquish it, instinctively comprehending that the state of surrender itself will be a creative condition.

It's hard to let go, to live in the formless, destinationless place. All our lives we're taught to hold on, to be the masters of our fate, the captains of our soul. Letting go isn't comfortable; it can feel like anything from laziness to utter loss of control. It's not aggressive and self-assured. It's not the American way.

But letting go is, in truth, a most elegant kind of daring. It is vulnerability of the highest order, an emptying out of the self, of all the clutter and chatter that, ordinarily, we all contain—ideas, attitudes, schemes, and plans—and offering your self as an empty vessel to be filled. In this emptiness, there is room for so much; in this vacancy, anything can happen: breathtaking transformations, changes of direction, miracles that will purely astound you, love that comes out of the woodwork, spiritual conversion.... But only if you are willing to truly let go of it all: as the tree dropping her bright leaves for winter, the trapeze artist, suspended in midair between the two bars, the diver free-falling from the high dive—have all unequivocally, wholeheartedly let go.

Letting go is being alive to the power of the nothingness. It is living in surrender, trust, and the belief that emptiness is at once the perfect completion and the perfect beginning. So let go. And remember that should you hang on to even a shred or try to make a deal with the gods ("I'll let go, but only if ..."), then nothing new—or wonderful—can happen. ✋

OFFER YOUR
LOVING SERVICE

*M*ost of the time we think of love in terms of what love can do for us, imagining that when we "fall in love," all our dreams will come true. We want so badly to have our own feelings recognized, our own needs met, our own insecurities handled, and our own desires fulfilled that the notion of love as service is almost inconceivable to us.

We can get so caught up (or bogged down) in the notion of love as a what-will-I-get-out-of-it experience that the idea of serving another is extremely distasteful. At a deeper level, we're afraid that by serving we might lose the sense of our selves we've worked so hard to attain. But in its purest state, love is service, a wholehearted offering so satisfying that it doesn't feel like service at all, but rather self-fulfillment of the highest order.

Most of us still need practice for this particular outreach of love. We're not sure how to serve or what our true service might be, and we haven't practiced serving to such a degree that it feels second nature, graceful, or effortless to us. The truth is that we're all already serving in one form or another. If you're a parent, you're serving your children. If you've cared for an invalid neighbor or an aging parent, you have also served in love. If you've bandaged the wing of a wounded bird, given a homeless person a dollar, saved a stranger from drowning, given up your seat on the subway, then you too have served in love. These are the seedlings of service, the places in which our hearts have started to open, but should you choose to have your service grow into a huge and sheltering tree, you will be given many opportunities to mature your gift of true service.

Begin by asking yourself the following questions: What does it mean to serve? What would my true service be? How can I develop my service so it can truly become a gift of love?

Service in love is temporarily setting aside your own needs, wants, and priorities and allowing the needs of another human being to become so radiant, so vivid, and so pertinent that, for a moment, your own are dissolved. This gracious moment is love, and the more we live in the practice of service, the more we create this love. For when we serve one another, we also serve the great cause of Love. ☙

CELEBRATE THE
"WE" OF YOU

*I*t is because in the "we" of union that the individual "I" becomes ever more beautifully defined that we enter into relationships in the first place. Somewhere, intuitively, we all know that love will make more of us than we ever would have become on our own. So without so much as a breathtaking pause, we "fall in love," give ourselves over to the charms of our beloved, and surrender ourselves to the mysteries of union.

Here everything changes. Through each nuance of behavior, whether a kiss, a conversation, the income taxes, or making love, you are asked to take account not only of your beloved, but also of your relationship. That's because when you fall in love, there's another spiritual entity—the "we," the "us"—that is brought into being. Although it's invisible, it is utterly alive—vibrant, vivid, and unique; continuously present as a discrete though subtle energetic essence. You can feel it when you're alone together as the mysterious unified play of your two energies. You can recognize it when you present yourselves to the world, as arm in arm you enter a room and create a wave of response. It's the constellation of ideas and points of view that, as a pair, you embody, the joy that, as a couple, you bring to all those around you. It is neither the sum of you both nor a negation of either of you. It is the mystical interaction by which an additional identity is created, where one plus one equals three, not two.

It is this entity—relationship, the embodiment of opposites attracting, then uniting; strangers gathered at the same hearth; lovers, together, under the stars, bidding good night to the day—that we are acknowledging when we speak of ourselves as a "couple," "Mr. and Mrs.," "my sweetheart and I," "we," or "us." "We had a wonderful time at the party." "It meant so much to *us* to go to Germany." And this entity, like the individuals in it, must also be nourished.

When you honor your relationship—by speaking adoringly of it to others, by treating your sexual relationship as a sacred bond, by standing fast together in times of turmoil and sorrow—you strengthen the power of your union. You nourish the "we" as the precious being it is, celebrate the unique, unrepeatable identity it has, and reweave the blanket of love that will warm and protect your union always. ✍

BE GRACEFUL, HOPEFUL,
AND WISE

*G*race is beauty of the spirit. Hope is the optimism of the soul, and wisdom is the soul's intelligence. These all are qualities of such eloquence that even as we hear the words, a quiet settles in our beings, as if from a far distant place we have heard once again the names of the elegant ancient virtues: Grace. Hope. Wisdom.

Grace, hope, and wisdom are all qualities of the soul. They refer to how our spirits operate in the world; they call up a sense of our deeper engagement with reality, and tell us again that, over, around, and through everything, a beautiful spiritual consciousness is quietly operating. So it is that grace adds a quality of silkiness to all our movements, not only to the way we move with our bodies, but to the way our spirits inhabit them; not only to the way we move through the world, but to the way in which, because of our genteel openness, we allow the world to move through us. Grace is beauty, refinement of the spirit. We feel it, recognize it, are beautifully softened and engaged by it, whenever we stand in its presence. In bringing us into its comeliness, grace brings us into our depth. We hold it as the measure of what we may longingly aspire to as the spiritual grandeur in our lives.

Hope is promise. When the present seems unbearable, hope allows us to live in the future and, there, to find ease. When we hope, we partake of the state of absolute calm that has already understood that everything we have done and everything we shall do, will be beautiful somewhere, sometime; that our sorrows will enhance us, that even our tragedies will bring us to our depth.

In wisdom we know without learning; we comprehend without effort. We remember what we were never told and can offer it, graciously, easily, as the truth that heals, the observation that clarifies, the intuition that illumines and brilliantly transforms. Wisdom is the soul's intelligence delivered, shared—the soul's ancient knowledge unselfconsciously revealed—in words that ring with the truth we have always known but never before been able to fully perceive.

Grace makes life fluid, flowing, and fine. Hope makes life lucky, exquisitely foreseen. And wisdom allows us to know when to trust grace and hope. Grace, wisdom, and hope are not shiny little virtues, but grand powers of the soul that will insist through their stunning magnificence that everything else in your life rise up to meet them. For when you cultivate grace, hope, and wisdom, they will require in every arena that you become much more than you already are, that you step through your old limitations and envision a larger world, a world breathtakingly beautiful, alive with possibility, and abundant with the power to truly redeem itself. ☺

LIVE IN THE LIGHT
OF THE SPIRIT

*W*ith each person who passes through your life, you have a soul agreement. What this means is that long ago, in the realm of the soul, you promised to have some special encounter, share some life-shaping experience, complete some soul-honing work with that particular soul in this life.

Soul agreements are commitments to the evolution of our individual souls in conjunction with one another, as one by one we make the journey to that state of seamless awareness that the mystics call "enlightenment." It is because of these agreements on a soul level that at times you may feel a mysteriously strange connection with some other person, why difficult people may at times inexplicably inhabit your life, why you may find yourself on a journey with a particular person—as if you had an unwritten contract to fulfill—and then discover that, as if by amputation, your association is suddenly over.

As the community of souls who have gathered together in life on Earth, we have agreed not only to remember for each other the pure state that was our origin, but also to act out whatever portion of the endlessly changing tableau of human experience we have been called upon to play to ensure our own soul's growth and that of the souls to whom we have made these deep promises. Some of us are here to be beautiful and strong, others to be cranky and difficult, some to die young and teach us through the searing heartbreak of great loss, others to live long and instruct us through wisdom. But no matter what role we are playing, we are all enacting a part in that one great spiritual destiny, which is to remember our eternal essence and move toward ultimate union.

So it is that every person you meet, each soul who crosses your path and affects you—wonderfully and terribly, briefly or for a lifetime—is here for that reason, and every relationship you engage in is but a small scene in the vast, ever-unfolding human panoply that is being endlessly enacted for the purpose of your soul's development. When you recognize this, you will suddenly, breathtakingly see that each person has been brought to you with a high and elegant purpose, that each soul has come to touch your soul and teach it, that each relationship exists to hasten your own soul's beautiful awakening. No longer is anyone a stranger; no longer can any of your relationships be seen as failures or mistakes.

In the light of the spirit, we see that we are all playing out roles that are the fulfillment of an exquisite and all-encompassing plan. To recognize this is to step out of conflict and into grace, for when we realize that life has been so beautifully designed, we will bask in the light of the spirit; we will live in absolute peace. ☺

ABOUT THE AUTHOR

For more than twenty-five years, Daphne Rose Kingma has worked as a psychotherapist whose practice has helped hundreds of individuals and couples understand and improve their relationships. Dubbed the "Love Doctor" by the *San Francisco Chronicle*, Daphne has appeared as a relationship expert on nationally broadcast television programs including *Oprah!*, *Sally Jessy Raphael*, and *The Leeza Gibbons Show*. The bestselling author of several books, including *Coming Apart*, *True Love*, *The Nine Types of Lovers*, and *Weddings from the Heart*, she lives in Santa Barbara, California.

If you would like to contact Daphne about speaking engagements you may write to her in care of:

New Directions
P. O. Box 5244
Santa Barbara, CA 93150